D1622227

Financial
and
Process Metrics
for the New Economy

Financial
and
Process Metrics
for the New Economy

James Sagner

AMACOM
American Management Association
New York • Atlanta • Boston • Chicago • Kansas City • San Francisco • Washington, D.C.
Brussels • Mexico City • Tokyo • Toronto

This publication is designed to provide accurate and authoritative information in regard to the subject matter covered. It is sold with the understanding that the publisher is not engaged in rendering legal, accounting, or other professional service. If legal advice or other expert assistance is required, the services of a competent professional person should be sought.

Library of Congress Cataloging-in-Publication Data

Sagner, James S.
    Financial and process metrics for the new economy / James Sagner.
        p.   cm.
    Includes bibliographical references and index.
    ISBN 0-8144-0600-9
    1. Electronic commerce.   I. Title.

HF5548.32.S18   2001
658.15—dc21

00-050223

Printing number

10   9   8   7   6   5   4   3   2   1

For **Claire** and **Benjamin**, for **Denali**, for **Molly**, who will
always be in our hearts, and for all the children to be

CONTENTS

LIST OF ILLUSTRATIONS

ACKNOWLEDGMENTS

I would like to thank the hundreds of clients and business friends from 20 years of consulting experience. I have learned far more from them than they have from me. To protect their confidentiality, I do not cite specific client names, and my discussion of companies in the book is based on public information sources.

Gratitude is expressed to the following individuals:

- Paula A. Lubas, CPA, who participated in the development of certain material in Part II of this book
- My former partner, Erik M. Bodow, CCM, who drafted an early version of the Gyzmo case for teaching purposes
- Ray O'Connell and Mike Sivilli of AMACOM, who guided this book through to publication

I appreciate the permission granted for the use of material that originally appeared as " 'Financial Metrics' for E-Commerce," *AFP Exchange*, Winter 2000, Vol. 20. © 2000 by the Association of Financial Professionals, all rights reserved. Certain other material originally appeared in our quarterly newsletter, *Treasury Views*, beginning in 1994.

Financial
and
Process Metrics
for the New Economy

INTRODUCTION

You will see something new.
Two things. And I call them
Thing One [financial metrics]
    and Thing Two [process metrics].

      —Dr. Seuss [Theodor Seuss Geisel] (1904–1991),
        The Cat in the Hat

This is a book about transaction finance and its component systems of analytics used in managing in the e-commerce new economy: financial and process metrics. "Financial metrics" are measures of income statement and balance sheet performance, usually expressed as the relationship of earnings or profits to sales, assets, or capital invested and adjusted for the "time value of money." "Process metrics" are measures of performance effectiveness and may be stated as the degree of completion of a task or work cycle element. Part I of the book addresses financial metrics, while Part II examines process metrics.

Financial Metrics

In today's financial markets, driven by earnings-per-share and price-earnings ratios, net profits have lost their usefulness to management to guide performance, initiate changes and corrective actions, and report to owners, managers, and the investment community. In the "dot.com" economy, there are often no earnings, and success is a function of the number of Website "hits" or "share of the market."

One of the reasons that the "earnings" metric is not informative is that it overlooks the impact of *time*. The duration of the transaction cycle must be considered in any business decision, but particularly given the e-commerce new economy requirement to react in "real-time." Our traditional tools of evaluation are more appropriate for the old economy—delay, review, analysis, debate, and consideration. Decision processes that might have taken weeks in

1970 or days in 1990 must now be completed in a few hours. In the future, you will have only minutes. If you make a mistake, your company may lose money, the goodwill of your customers and suppliers, and the esteemed position that may have taken years to attain.

What is suggested are meaningful financial metrics to evaluate opportunities in the new business environment. These metrics include the standard return ratios—return on sales and return on equity—as well as the gross margin percentage. However, we adjust our calculations in a time value of money calculation.

Process Metrics

Process metrics are the determinants of sub-optimal manufacturing and non-manufacturing processes and result directly in inefficient work-day cycles. It is critical for twenty-first-century companies to chart and evaluate performance factors over time, to control against adverse changes influencing organizational performance. Financial metrics differ from process metrics in that the underlying data of the former are required by the Securities and Exchange Commission and various other regulators. Process metrics either are not charted, or are made meaningless through benchmarking or "best practices."

Benchmarking or "best practices" is used to compare the performance of competitors, usually by a statistical determination of superior (i.e., fifth quintile), average (i.e., mean), and inferior (i.e., first quintile) performance in a sample of, say, 30 or 50 "equivalent" companies. Best practice/benchmarking reviews generally fall into one of two categories:

- *Ratio Comparisons*. These assess productivity by measuring how much is produced (the output) against resources consumed (the input).
- *Checklists of Practices*. This approach uses a checklist of practices other companies follow. Best practices can often be identified with such checklists by correlating the practices followed to that of "top performers."

While this approach generally is goal oriented and quantitative, it is somewhat simple-minded, ignores complex qualitative concerns, and unrealistically assumes the comparability of complex organizations. Instead, we use process metrics as a set of longitudinal (i.e., over time) measures for the individual company, which, by definition, is a unique entity. These measures assist in the identification of problems that result in sub-optimal financial metric results. Process metrics are measured in days, units, or percentages.

The Significance of Time

Time is a critical metric because work-days can be converted to a value called "float" and any improvement opportunity calculated at the cost of capital. Let's use the example of the automobile industry. The "old economy" manufacturing and delivery cycle has typically required 57 days for a made-to-order vehicle; see Exhibit A-1. "New economy" auto makers expect to reduce this time to 14 days. The value of the time saved (at a 10% cost of capital) is $300 for a $25,000 car.[1] Applied to half a million cars, that's $150 million!

Furthermore, the faster time to deliver a car translates to more satisfied customers, fewer cars financed and sitting on dealer lots awaiting sale, and in general a more efficient approach to business. To accomplish this, numerous small adjustments are being implemented, including tracking each car shipped to expedite delivery, communicating with suppliers using electronic commerce, limiting some options on vehicles to move toward economic order quantity, and fostering two-way communications with dealers to improve the sales/production cycle. (All of these process metric changes are discussed in Part II.) The critical concept in these improvement efforts is the management of time.

Electronic Commerce

There are tens of thousands of Websites for electronic commerce (or e-commerce) and the new economy. Depending on the source quoted, the market potential in the next five years or so will be in the billions or trillions of dollars. A minority view—and our opin-

1. Calculated as $25,000 divided by 360 days times (57 days less 14 days) times 10%.

Exhibit A-1. Total days to manufacture and ship an automobile.

Cycles	Old Economy Days	New Economy Days	Explanation
Ordering:	7	1	Batch and forward special car orders; expedited by computer entry at time of order
Manufacturing	28	4	Produce cars with numerous combinations of options; accelerated by use of packaged options
Shipping	20	8	Transport cars by rail; improved tracking of vehicles for improved routing
Final preparation	2	1	Preparing unsold rather than sold cars for delivery; changed emphasis on sold cars to improve customer service
Total days	57	14	

Source: Keith Bradsher, "The Long, Long Wait for Cars," *New York Times,* May 9, 2000, pp. C1, C29.

ion—is that billions of dollars will be spent (and consumed) before any real economic value is developed for the global business community. For example, a recent analysis of the "burn" rate of publicly traded Internet stocks (with a total market capitalization of $1.3 trillion) shows that one-fourth will exhaust their cash within one year.[2]

Meanwhile, companies and investors are leaping into electronic

2. Jack Willoughby, "Burning Up," *Barron's*, March 20, 2000, pp. 29–32.

commerce without carefully considering the ramifications of new economy business practices. When it does take hold, e-commerce will threaten the survival of established corporations, particularly old economy companies, which have been moderately efficient, indifferent to their true costs, and content to enjoy profitability from the limited competition in their prevailing economic structure—oligopoly. This is all going to change as a result of:

- Real global competition
- The decline of traditional buyer/seller relationships
- Financial impacts—the realization of the actual costs of labor, materials, overhead, and capital

Geographic Focus

Although the discussion in the book is global, our primary concern in these early years of e-commerce is U.S. business. The new economy transformation has been primarily an American phenomenon, as has been much of the development of e-commerce. In fact, a recent survey of readiness for e-business, carried out by *The Economist* magazine, showed the U.S. as the leader, as determined by the general business environment and communications infrastructure. The Scandinavian countries ranked next, and Japan was the lowest ranked G-7 country.[3]

However, this is not necessarily good news for American companies. There is a clear tendency in this country to develop and commercialize technology without a real understanding of the ramifications for management, finance, and customer and vendor relationships. The outstanding example is probably the nuclear energy industry (referenced again in the final chapter), but other similar situations include the computer, semiconductor, and cellular telephone industries, all good news, and the aluminum electrical wiring, asbestos building insulation, and hydrogen dirigible industries, all bad news. International companies will learn from U.S. experience and avoid the inevitable fiascos.

3. Issue of June 3–June 9, 2000, cited at its Website, www.economist.com.

Structure of the Book

This book is organized into three sections to present financial metrics (Part I), process metrics (Part II), and conclusions (Part III). We begin Part I with a description of the old and the new economies and then develop our approach to transaction finance. The device of the Gyzmo case is used to describe manufacturing, marketing, and administrative issues. Gyzmo is based on our experiences with several clients and includes a comprehensive discussion of "old" and "new" economy issues, supported by financial statements, an organization chart, the bank account structure, and other information.

We continue Gyzmo in Part II to work through the specific components of manufacturing cost: materials purchasing, work-in-process, the invoicing cycle, and the receipt of good funds. We also discuss issues relating to service industries, sales and marketing, and general and administrative costs. This is not a detailed cost accounting presentation; rather, the intention is to present "old" and "new" economy approaches to the management and measurement of the transaction cycle. This section concludes with an afterword, summarizing the process metric discussion.

The book concludes in Part III with comments on the development of new economy businesses in the next decade—who will be the "winners" and who will be the "losers." Brief chapter appendixes are inserted at appropriate places in the book to amplify important concepts. This supplement format is used to avoid interrupting the flow of the text and because of the multifaceted nature of the coverage of new economy financial metrics. The appendices are included in Chapter 2 on economic concentration; Chapter 3 on the time value of money; Chapter 5 on Internet security; Chapter 7 on manufacturing and supply chain management; and Chapter 12 on enterprise resource planning and XML. In addition, there is an appendix to the book in which is listed companies that will successfully function as e-commerce facilitators.

Part I

Financial Metrics and the Old and New Economies

I wonder what goes on in this job?

Financial metrics are used to evaluate income statement and balance sheet returns as adjusted for "time value of money" considerations. Chapters 1 and 2 discuss the old and new economies, Chapter 3 defines financial metrics, and Chapters 4 and 5 demonstrate these metrics in the context of the Gyzmo case.

Chapter 1

THE OLD ECONOMY

And slowly answer'd Arthur from the barge:
The old order changeth, yielding place to new . . .

—Alfred, Lord Tennyson (1809–1892),
The Idylls of the King

Since the beginning of the Industrial Revolution, the "old" economy has consisted of labor- and/or capital-intensive industries and companies. In the next two chapters we contrast and compare the demands for meaningful financial metrics in the old economy and the so-called new economy.

Old Economy Business Strategy

The business strategies developed in the old economy have been sustained by a mix of manufacturing processes, distribution channels, price, customer service, efficiencies in managing costs, information technology, and other significant product features. Despite the intensive search for the special factor or cause of business prosperity,[1] each success is the result of a unique selling proposition or idea that was cleverly developed, executed, and promoted.

Companies achieved their strategic position through a variety of circumstances. These include invention (Xerox), the attainment of optimal scale economies (the integrated oil companies), capital barriers to entry (the international airlines), regulatory protection (public utilities), proprietary information (insurance), or long-established customer relationships (commercial banks).

Relationship (or "reach," to use the Evans and Wurster term[2])

1. See, for example, James C. Collins and Jerry I. Porras, *Built to Last* (New York: HarperBusiness, 1994).
2. Philip Evans and Thomas S. Wurster, *Blown to Bits* (Boston: Harvard Business School Press, 1999), Chapter 6.

has been one of the most potent of these strategic advantages, because trust in a brand or corporate image allows customers to avoid continuously searching for the optimal combination of price and product. Such searches are costly, inconvenient, and not at all certain to produce optimal results.

Many corporate transactions are so complicated that intermediaries function to aid the process. The intermediary may take title to the product (e.g., a wholesaler) or may be an agent or broker who typically does not take title (e.g., insurance agents). Whenever intermediaries function in a business marketplace, there have been years of market position and expertise to establish and sustain that role.

Certain companies (e.g., Disney) have managed to retain their primacy for generations by combining a unique selling proposition, innovation in distribution channels, and uninspired competition. Others fail to exploit their tactical advantages and disappear (Wang Computers) or are merged into another organization (the computer business of Honeywell). The continual re-invention or re-engineering of the corporation has been necessary for survival; when it is stimulated and fostered by the insight of senior management, permanence is likely.

However, many venerable organizations may become too tradition-bound to improve or innovate and are often forced to carry a legacy set of "resources" that can be more of a drag than an asset. These companies may have been constrained by a strategy that emphasized premium pricing (e.g., the pharmaceutical industry), distribution channels that are too limiting (e.g., consumer products sold door-to-door or at "parties"), or a failure to continuously innovate on the original concept (e.g., Kodak). These mistakes can lead to permanent changes in the viability of the company or an industry.

Old Economy Business Structure

A functional organization structure has traditionally been used to manage in old economy companies, with the "line" functions of sales and production separated from the "staff" (or advisory) functions of finance, information, and other administrative elements. Each function tends to operate within its own boundaries and time frames, so long as these constraints are convenient to the mission of the business.

Rules govern the conduct of each business function in these companies. There are rules for a sale, for granting credit, for issuing an invoice, for accepting late payment, for paying bills and payroll, and so forth. Exceptions generally have to be approved by an experienced manager. When mistakes are made, leading to losses or marginal profits, the manager (one hopes) learns from the misjudgment and has the time to acclimate his or her thinking to meet the next situation. All of this is measured by traditional return-on-sales (ROS) or return-on-equity (ROE) criteria, as measured by accounting concepts that have their roots in fifteenth-century Italy.[3]

The structures that manage old economy organizations have been repeatedly criticized for their bureaucratic character, including hierarchy of authority (e.g., reporting to a single manager), formality, and rigidity. Various schemes have been suggested to increase flexibility, speed decision-making, and foster innovation, including matrixed structures, where workers can report to various managers depending on specific business requirements, and flat organizations, where workers take the responsibility for managing themselves without constant supervisory review. However, the centuries-old model of line-and-staff continues as the predominant structure.

Old Economy Assumptions

Old economy companies make several somewhat unrealistic assumptions, given twenty-first-century business practice.

The Profit Factor Continuum

With slight adjustments for inflation, old economy companies assume a constancy in the occurrence of similar sales and cost factors. However, we know that terms of sales, price discounts, and promotional rebates often vary by customer and that costs may fluctuate

---

3. The first accounting text is generally acknowledged to be *Summa de Arithmetica, Geometrica. Proportioni et Proportionalita*, by Luca Pacioli (1494).

due to changes in manufacturing processes, variations in materials costs, or other causes.

We compensate for changes in expense factors by various artificial accounting procedures, such as "LIFO" (last-in, first-out) costing of inventory and sum-of-the-years digits to accelerate depreciation for capital equipment. However, we cannot realistically expect any accounting routine or any forecast, no matter how insightful, to anticipate how customers, products, or processes will behave in a dynamic market.

Actual Margins Meet Target Objectives

With recurring sales and cost factors, we expect to make business forecasts with a large measure of reliability. We can never know that we will sell 1,000 widgets in Year 2, or that it will cost $50 to make each widget, but in the old economy, these targets can be projected with the assumption that we'll be within 10 or 20% of actual experience. However, returns now fluctuate significantly from forecasts because of a variety of exogenous factors not foreseeable when projects are initiated, including general economic conditions and the response of global competitors.

Immateriality of the Time Value of Money.

The time value of money (TVM) concept means that a dollar earned or spent today is worth more than one earned in the future. However, the usual calculation of profits in ongoing business operations does not account for this adjustment, and currency units are not adjusted for TVM. TVM is used almost exclusively in capital budgeting decisions involving multiyear flows of cash to acquire equipment or similar assets. Typical procedures include "net present value" and "internal rate of return"; these are discussed in the Chapter 3 appendix.

The "building block" of corporate finance is the cost of capital, which is the weighted cost of debt and equity used to support a company's capital structure.[4] The low cost of capital experienced

---

4. The components of the cost of capital include the after-tax cost of debt capital and the cost of equity capital, measured as the expected growth rate of a company's profits or stock price plus the dividend yield (also known as the "total return").

until the 1970s (about 6%) has vanished. We can use 1965 as the border between the era of low interest rates and the period of escalating interest rates, driven largely by the decision of the Johnson administration to fund its spending on the Vietnam War by deficit spending rather than tax increases. From 1955 to 1964 midyear short-term interest rates (as measured by federal funds) averaged 2.5%, but then began an escalation that now has rates at about 5.5%; see Exhibit 1-1.

Although interest rates are down from their highs (reached at the time of the OPEC oil embargo of the 1970s, they reflect what has occurred generally in the financial markets: capital costs that are one and one-half to two times those of the post–World War II era. The soaring stock market may enrich most of us, but it does tremendously increase the cost of equity capital.[5] A typical Y2K corporation could have a cost of capital of 12%, and many companies have costs as high as 14–16%. See Exhibit 1-2.

These are not trivial costs for any business, and appear to constitute a permanent change in the cost of financing a business. Even

Exhibit 1-1. Average interest rates.

	Federal Funds*	Long-Term U.S. Treasury Securities**
1955–1964	2.51%	3.69%
1965–1974	6.82%	5.67%
1975–1984	9.64%	9.69%
1985–1994	6.26%	8.30%
1995–1999	5.46%	6.47%

Rates shown are from midyear.
*Federal funds ("fed funds") are deposits held by commercial banks at the Federal Reserve. The federal funds rate is the interest rate at which these funds are traded, usually on an overnight basis. It is a standard benchmark for short-term interest rates in the U.S., similar to LIBOR (London Interbank Offered Rate) on Eurodollar deposits.
**Treasury long-term bond yields are the unweighted average of yields on all issues of bonds outstanding that are neither due nor callable in less than 10 years.
Source: Calculated from data provided in www.federalreserve.gov/releases/H15/data/m/fed fund.txt.

5. Stock market data are more difficult to uncover. One authority notes that the decade of the 1960s averaged 8.17% on a total return basis, versus about 20% for the past two years, an increase of nearly 250%! See www.globalfindata.com/april.htm. See also Ibbotson Staff, *Stocks, Bonds, Bills and Inflation Yearbook: Market Results for 1926–1999*, Dominic Falaschetti and Michael Annin, eds., published annually.

though inflation is mild (except for episodes of oil price increases, war, or other temporary incidents), the markets now expect a significant return for "hired" capital, regardless of whether it is by a loan or a share of ownership.

Customer/Vendor Delays

Old economy companies generally follow established business standards regarding the timing of billing, collection, and payables. Consistent with practice in its industry, a company may establish terms of "2/10, n/30." This means that a cash discount of 2% is allowed if payment is received within 10 days of the invoice date, and payment in full is expected by day 30. Some industries offer other terms, such as net 30 (no discounting); or 1/10, n/30; or 2/20, n/30. Similar types of terms are offered and followed for payables. New economy companies pay bills when they have the cash, and since

Exhibit 1-2. Calculation of old and new economy corporate cost of capital.

	Portion of Balance Sheet	*Pretax Costs*	*After-Tax Costs*	*Component Costs (a)*
Old Economy Cost of Capital				
Debt	40%	.045	.030 (b)	.012
Equity	60%	.085 (c)	.085	.050
Total	100%			.062
New Economy Cost of Capital				
Debt	40%	.090	.060 (b)	.024
Equity	60%	.160 (d)	.160	.096
Total	100%			.120

a. Portion of Balance Sheet times After-Tax Costs.
b. Assumes 34% corporate tax rate.
c. Assumes 6% growth + $2\frac{1}{2}$% dividend.
d. Assumes 12% growth + 4% dividend.

they often wait 45 days or more for their invoices to be paid,[6] credit terms have deteriorated 50% or more.

Business Unit Delays

Business units in a company focus on the requirements of their specified functional responsibilities, without full consideration for the needs of the organization.

- A sales function is motivated and tasked to sell, without regard to the profitability of the transaction; the impact of promises made to customers on manufacturing, quality control, and shipping; or whether the customer will pay on time (or ever!).
- An information systems function protects its computing resources and may be oblivious to the optimal timing of invoicing, upgrading systems serving customer service functions, or the needs of management to access management information it can use.

Business unit managers are inattentive to the needs of the organization because it's not in their performance objectives; instead, dollars of sales or standards of systems performance are the criteria by which they're evaluated.

Enterprise Delays

For the past 20 years, we have worked with clients to review their management of the "cashflow timeline." The timeline is a graphic presentation of the events along a continuum from the first activity in the sales cycle until the final disbursement of funds for accounts payable, payroll, or other outflow requirements.

Every major organization we've observed (some 200 of the Fortune 500) has significant timeline delays. These may be attributable

---

6. Published statistics on days sales outstanding (DSO), which represent actual bill paying experience, indicate that practice varies from about 30 to about 60 days, depending on the industry, with average DSO at about 45 days. For data on DSO, see Dun & Bradstreet's Website www. dnb.com.

to billing lags due to systems "priorities" or incomplete data, inefficiencies in receiving and depositing cash receipts, delayed posting to accounts receivable, archaic banking systems, overly aggressive accounts payable systems, or other factors.

Improvements to the timeline require the re-configuration of cash events, involving:

• *Establishing Alternative Scenarios.* In a financial environment, a "scenario" is a statement of outcomes with regard to a significant portion of the cashflow timeline. Scenarios involve permutations of internal processing, outsourcing, or some combination.

• *Quantifying the Scenarios.* The process of quantifying the scenarios involves the determination of each cost element inherent in completing the cashflow events.

• *Creating a Scenario Impact Table.* A scenario impact table graphically presents the findings from the process of scenario quantification and assists in the selection of the optimal outcome.[7]

How Old Economy Companies Muddle Through

The aggregated impact of unrealistic assumptions often is to convert a profitable business activity to one with marginal returns or even losses. Let's examine how that can occur. Our target ROS is 10% to make a 15% ROE, and we sell widgets for $100 at a target cost of $90 in a processing cycle of 90 days. However, it actually takes 60 days to produce, ship, and invoice and another 42 days for the customer to pay.[8] By the time we receive "good" funds in our bank, another six days have passed,[9] for a total of 108 days.

The 18 days we did not forecast is 20% greater the target (90 days), which drives the ROS to 8% and the ROE to 12%. An ROE of 12% is well above our cost of capital of 6% in the old economic order but about equal to our cost of capital in the new economy. In the old economy, we could tolerate this situation as we would expect to

7. For a complete discussion of these procedures, see James S. Sagner, *Cashflow Reengineering* (New York: AMACOM, 1997).
8. This is explained in Chapters 6, 7, and 9.
9. This is explained in Chapter 10.

correct our 18-day overrun in later operations. We will see in subsequent chapters whether this period of adjustment is permitted in the new economy.

From this example, for every $1 million of product sold, each extra day of delay costs the company (and the economic system) about $1,000.[10] Our research with clients indicates that the average delay is about five days. With the business component of the U.S. economy some $6.4 trillion, or 75% of total Gross Domestic Product,[11] a rough forecast measure of the inefficiency of the U.S. economy exceeds $30 billion annually! (Of course, this assumes that all U.S. businesses are equally inefficient, which we sincerely hope is not the case.)

In fact, many businesses have long accepted these lapses as a cost of doing business. They experience discontinuous intervals of mediocre results but use such outcomes to trigger adjustments to delays and inefficiencies. Modifications may be made at any point in the business timeline and may involve a production process, the terms of sale, the financial arrangements for the transaction, or any of a nearly limitless number of variables. Managers may not be able to quantify the days or costs of delay, but they eventually discover that the target ROS and ROE are not being met. In this way, corrective action is taken to return to expected returns.[12]

It is critical to acknowledge the iterative process of old economy management. Business managers learn their profession in the same way as attorneys, physicians, and other professionals: by training under the supervision of experienced practitioners using the most current set of analytical tools and procedures. Mistakes are expected, because it's part of human nature to err. In the old economy there is always time to correct an error.

10. Calculated as 2% of $1 million divided by 18 days.
11. For business non-farm GDP excluding housing and government, U.S. Department of Commerce, *Economic Report of the President*, 1999, Table B-10.
12. A popular concept beginning in 1960s management literature was "management-by-exception," which advocated establishing control limits for production processes. Any result outside those limits must be examined to initiate corrective action. See, for example, Paul E. Torgersen and Irwin T. Weinstock, *Management: An Integrated Approach* (New York: Prentice-Hall, 1972), Chapter 20.

When Muddling Through Doesn't Work

Serious problems obviously arise where corrective action is not taken. Unfortunately, this happens all too often in business for several reasons.

B-I-G Business

The modern corporation has become so large and diversified that no one individual can oversee all of its activities. While the CEO may be briefed on sales, profits, and product developments by sector or market, a Fortune 500 company may simply be too complex to manage in any sense of controlling the company's use of scarce factors of production. We often find that our clients do not understand their own businesses, do not adequately calculate profitability, and cannot relate the activities in one business unit to those in another unit.

Senior management frequently is managing a portfolio of investments, much as if they were running an equity mutual fund. Often, those in charge were trained in completely different businesses (e.g., Louis Gerstner Jr. at IBM, who came from RJR Nabisco and American Express, or Leo Mullin at Delta Air Lines, formerly at the First National Bank of Chicago). Or they learned to run a smaller company that was manageable to an informed and energetic CEO but then are unable to succeed in the colossal version (e.g., John B. McCoy at BankOne).[13]

The most extreme case of B-I-G business mismanagement in recent years may well be "Chainsaw" Al Dunlop, who left Scott Paper (now part of Kimberly Clark) to become CEO of the Sunbeam Corporation. Dunlap eliminated 12,000 employees, closed scores of plants, made three ill-advised acquisitions, and allowed significant misstatements of earnings to hype the company's stock price. In his two years at Sunbeam, he nearly destroyed the brand, demoralized employees, and lost millions of dollars. In the end, he was forced out as a series of class actions lawsuits was being filed on behalf of investors.

13. For a discussion of the BankOne situation, principally problems at the First USA credit card unit, see "Cracks in the Wall at Bank One," *Business Week*, December 13, 1999, p. 164. McCoy resigned on December 19.

Inadequate Measures of Profitability

It is nearly impossible to match costs to sales in order to accurately determine profits. Generally accepted accounting principles (GAAP) allow considerable leeway in the statement of business income. "Accrual accounting" assigns costs to the timing of the sale of product, rather than to the time that the cost was incurred, and recognizes sales at the time of invoicing, rather than at the time that funds are received.[14]

Both the nature of accrual accounting and permitted leeway in the interpretation of the recording of business events allow companies to report earnings that may not accurately reflect economic results. More than 80% of the 30 companies in the Dow Jones Industrial Average incurred restructuring charges between 1991 and 1995.[15] By suppressing current profits, these costs tend to enhance future earnings, and stock prices respond accordingly. An example is IBM, where re-structuring charges were $6.3 billion *more* than reported profits during the 1991–1995 period. These types of charges make it nearly impossible to know "true" earnings at any given time.

Occasionally, accounting data are not only misleading but fraudulent. Traditionally, the accounting profession has provided independent audits of financial records and opinions as to the accuracy of the financial statements presented by the business enterprise. It has never been the accountant's objective to search out and report instances of fraud or to otherwise provide warning of any potential problems for the subject of their audit.

Auditors provide carefully worded opinions regarding the extent of their responsibilities and investigations. Typical language is: "These financial statements are the responsibility of the company's management. Our responsibility is to express an opinion on the statements based on our audits." As audits are currently performed, it is fairly clear that a clever fraud will not be detected by the external auditor. Even when fraud has been detected, auditors have resigned from clients but are under no compulsion to publicly disclose the reasons.

14. "Cash accounting," which recognizes sales and costs at the time when cash is received or spent, is used primarily by small businesses.
15. "Reviewing Restructurings: What the Disclosures Show," *The Analyst's Accounting Observer*, Vol. 5, No. 9, August 23, 1996.

The rise in fraud was acknowledged by three-fourths of the corporate respondents in a KPMG Peat Marwick survey, with *each* fraud exceeding $1 million.[16] Financial statement frauds include recording sales before earned or shifting expenses to later periods, creating fictitious income, hiding liabilities, and similar actions.[17]

The Wrong Performance Measure

Managers are often motivated through objectives or measures that emphasize their own business unit needs but are not entirely consistent with the goals of the company. If we are managing an accounts payable unit, our goal may be to handle invoices expeditiously, rather than to release payments at the proper time or after a complete review of purchase orders and receiving reports.

In any sales function the focus is on the sale and not on the profit generated by that sale. Few businesses tie manufacturing, sales, and administrative costs to specific sales, and even fewer have any idea whether a particular sale, product, or market generates appropriate profits. Accounting treatment of unit costs has historically been oriented to production and not to marketing, and the job of the cost accountant is to tell us to the tenth of a penny the cost to manufacture a "widget."

Profits are critical to the enterprise, but the concept has little meaning to the individual manager because of the difficulty of calculating the appropriate allocation of non-direct organizational costs to specific business units. The manager often has very imprecise data on which to judge the profitability of his or her product, service, or business line and little input into the process of assigning costs against revenues.

Furthermore, although certain cost elements are variable in the long-run and therefore subject to some control, nearly all costs are fixed in the short run. For example, labor is usually considered as a variable direct cost, yet hiring, transfer, and termination decisions are subject to various contractual and legislated restrictions.

16. Reported in W. M. Michaelson, "In Search of Hidden Assets," *The Practical Accountant*, February 1995, pp. 39–45.
17. See Howard M. Schilit, *Financial Shennanigans: How to Detect Accounting Gimmicks & Fraud in Financial Reports* (New York: McGraw-Hill, 1993).

Let's Fix the Organization

Faced with the huge growth of their businesses, old economy companies often reorganize by strategic business units (SBUs) or profit
centers to encourage entrepreneurship and a focus on ROE. However, this approach can create artificial barriers (commonly known
as "silos") to the sharing of important resources, customer data, and
sales opportunities, and can result in redundant financial and information systems and distribution channels.

- A large financial services company encouraged the development of customer systems by each of its business units, without the
benefit of input from and use of the expertise of the other businesses. The approach resulted in redundant human, computer, and
systems resources and an inability to share databases on customers,
competitors, and vendors. In this situation, a business unit selling a
financial product into one market would not be able to help another
business unit of the same parent company sell a complementary
product.

- In a high-tech manufacturing company, each business unit
developed its own customer invoicing and receivables systems. Although there were customers who were common to the various
business units, the company could not access their data to determine payment terms, contract arrangements, or collection histories.
A customer with good credit in one SBU was considered a poor
credit risk in another SBU!

SBUs or silos lead to polarization in terms of customer relations
and sales and facilitate employee politics rather than cooperation.
In simple terms, it becomes "us" versus "them." In the spirit of
"competition," senior management effectively discourages cooperation. The result is secrecy, rather than the sharing of information.

You can tell if an old economy company has the silo mentality
by asking a few questions of management:

- Is a dictionary needed to understand the acronyms and al-
  phabet soup describing the company's systems?
- Do workers refer to their employer as the business unit,
  rather than the company, as in "I work for the Superior Division," rather than "I work for the Gigantic Corporation"?

- Do sales people from different business units find themselves competing for the same piece of business?
- Do operations people from these units tend to communicate and socialize only within their businesses, rather than with people throughout the organization?
- Are there multiple layers of systems support (e.g., corporate, division, and/or business unit)?
- Are staff functions (e.g., finance, human resources, law) considered the enemy by line managers?
- Does senior management seem to be operating the company as a portfolio of investments, rather than as an integrated whole?

The Real Challenge to the Old Economy

Despite declarations proclaiming the demise of the old economy,[18] to quote Mark Twain, "The reports of my death are greatly exaggerated."[19] Some companies experience the worst of management and survive (e.g., Sunbeam, but barely), and some do not (e.g., Wang). There is no real prospect of any global economy forgoing the traditional necessities of life—food, clothing, shelter, transportation, healthcare, national security—for Internet access, financial investments, or scientific discoveries. Instead, for the indefinite future, we will continue to require the products and services provided by the old economy. And, although we're inefficient, perhaps to an amount measured in the tens of billions of dollars in the U.S., as discussed earlier, the economy gets the job done at a cost we've been willing to accept. The disruption to the old economy comes from a feature of the new economy that business has never before encountered: the requirement for real-time decision-making. In the next chapter we discuss the characteristics and challenges of the new economy and the inadequacies of our fifteenth-century accounting "information."

18. See, for example, "The Prosperity Gap," *Business Week*, September 27, 1999, pp. 90–102.
19. Cable from London to the Associated Press, 1897. Twain (Samuel L. Clemens) died in 1910.

Chapter 2

THE NEW ECONOMY

The new electronic interdependence recreates the world in the image of a global village.

—Marshall McLuhan (1911–1980),
The Medium Is the Massage

The new economy comprises organizations founded on intellectual capital, where investment is not in plant and equipment but in information systems, patents and copyrights, people and ideas. The change to a "thought" product focus from the manufactured-product focus of the old economy causes particular difficulties in the development of useful financial metrics. The eventual undoing of the established corporate order could result.

What Is the New Economy?

Descriptions of the twenty-first-century new economy variously focus on macroeconomic changes, corporate governance, and/or Internet connectivity. Commentators use the concept of the new economy to explain various developing trends and elements that differ from our old economy experiences of the past three centuries. These include:

- The irrelevance of the business cycle[1]
- Changes to the corporation in terms of organizational form and the development of business strategy[2]

1. See various *Business Week* articles beginning in 1998, for example, Michael J. Mandel, "Handling the Hot-Rod Economy," July 12, 1999, pp. 30–31. Or see Jeff Madrick, "How New Is the New Economy?" *New York Review of Books*, September 23, 1999, pp. 42–50.
2. See, for example, Philip Evans and Thomas S. Wurster, *Blown to Bits* (Boston: Harvard Business School Press, 1999), or Douglas F. Aldrich, *Mastering the Digital Marketplace* (New York: John Wiley & Sons, 1999).

- The role of politics and government in a technological society[3]
- New economy workplace and labor market issues[4]
- The impact of the Internet on business transactions[5]

In short, there is no general agreement on precisely what the new economy is, how it will function, and what will be its impact on management and its various constituencies.[6]

The fact that there are issues of definition has not dampened the mad rush to participate in the new economy through the medium of electronic commerce ("e-commerce") or business-to-business (B2B). According to data compiled by *Business Week* from various sources,[7] annual sales using e-commerce will be $1.5 trillion and 91% of U.S. business will purchase from Internet sources by 2004, five times the consumer e-commerce market. Average efficiencies from e-commerce applications could be as much as 12.5%; see Exhbit 2-1 for estimates of cost savings by industry.

Focus of the New Economy

In a macroeconomic sense, old economy growth assumptions may be discarded in favor of higher growth, larger national government budget surpluses, and less intervention by the central bank (in the U.S., the Federal Reserve).[8] Lower unemployment rates may be accepted without fearing inflation, and anticipated budget surpluses

3. See, for example, Diane Coyle, *The Weightless World* (Cambridge, Mass.: MIT Press, 1998).
4. See, e.g., Stephen A. Herzenberg, John A. Alic, and Howard Wial, *New Rules for a New Economy* (Ithaca, N.Y.: Cornell University Press, 1998).
5. See, e.g., Kevin Kelly, *New Rules for the New Economy* (New York: Viking, 1998).
6. However, there is certainly no shortage of jargon. For example, consider Evans and Wurster's "deconstruction" or "navigators"; Kelly's "embrace the swarm" and "follow the free"; Aldrich's "digital function platform" and "value-based organization."
7. "B2B: The Hottest Net Bet Yet?" January 17, 2000, pp. 36–37. Boston Consulting Group estimates that the value of business-to-business e-commerce transactions will be $2 trillion by 2003; see their Website, www.bcg.com.
8. Old economy assumptions considered Gross Domestic Product growth in excess of 2.5–3.0% to be inflationary and unsustainable. New economy estimates allow non-inflationary growth of 3.0–3.5%.

Exhibit 2-1. E-commerce cost savings by industry grouping.

Aerospace machining	11%	Healthcare	5%
Chemicals	10%	Life sciences	12–19%
Coal	2%	Metals machining	22%
Communications	5–15%	Media/advertising	10–15%
Computing	11–20%	Maintenance/repair/ operating supplies	10%
Electronic components	29–39%		
Food ingredients	3–5%	Oil/gas	5–15%
Forest products	15–25%	Paper	10%
Freight transport	15–20%	Steel	11%

Source: Goldman Sachs.
Reprinted from "B2B: The Hottest Net Bet Yet?" *Business Week,* January 17, 2000, pp. 36–37, by special permission, copyright © 2000 by The McGraw-Hill Companies, Inc.

can be used to reduce the national debt to stabilize long-term rates of interest. Economic growth is also supported by continuing investment in technology to boost productivity, and by recovery and development of the global economy. Interestingly, commentators are silent on the dollar/euro/yen relationship: do we support a stronger or a weaker dollar in the new economy?

The strategy of the new economy will be to compete globally in industries that emphasize intellectual property, as opposed to a manufactured product emphasis of the old economy. Instead of counting raw material inputs of coal, sand, and iron ore, or labor inputs of manual and skilled labor, we will be using data and technology to produce information systems, financial services, and scientific discoveries. The industrial groups emphasized in the new economy include computers, stock brokerages and banking, media and telecommunications, consulting, and medicine and the health professions. In summary, we will be *thinking* as opposed to *producing*.

People and Physical Resources

Wages in the new economy will grow up to four times faster than those in the old economy on the basis of exponential gains in the speed of computer processing. Workers will be continually reassigned to projects and groups, with a natural migration to information and technology-based jobs. The concepts of a lifetime career, employer-employee loyalty, or a company retirement program will become obsolete, and, in effect, the worker often "fires" the employer!

The most valuable resource in the new economy is the intellect and creativity of the worker and his or her group, and the corporation must pay the market rate for those skills in much the same way that professional athletes or entertainers sell their services to the highest bidder. The concept of the worker as a cog in an industrial economy (cf., Charlie Chaplin in *Modern Times*) becomes irrelevant; in fact, the skilled worker is a very prized and somewhat independent asset. As a result, private-sector union membership in the U.S. has declined to the position it held in 1900 (less than 10% of workers), and the labor movement is struggling to defend its deteriorating role.

The proportion of production workers declined from about three-fourths of all workers in 1900 to about one-fourth of all workers at the start of the twenty-first century. We no longer depend on sweatshops to produce manufactured goods; today, the majority of workers are involved in customer service, administration, or technological services. The recognition of intellectual capital has empowered the individual worker, who enjoys recognition, training, and promotions on the basis of his or her knowledge.

With intellect of primary importance, the value of physical assets has diminished, and management now tries to minimize the fixed asset portion of the balance sheet and the need to raise capital. Those valuable fixed assets that companies own cannot be measured by traditional accounting: besides human capital, the inherent knowledge in the corporate culture and relationships with suppliers and customers developed over years of interactions.

In this environment, our traditional assumptions about economic behavior and scarce resources are no longer correct. When we use up an asset in the old economy, it's gone; in the new economy, the theory is that it expands as *information* and continually creates new benefits. One innovation leads to others, and the aggregate is greater than the resources used to create it. Old economics rewards the sale of products for more than their cost of manufacture and marketing; new economics accepts losses to both capture market share and drive down future costs on the basis of learning curve insight.

Global Applicability

The application of new economy principles has focused primarily on the U.S., largely because of the dominance of its economy. In addition, there are significant cultural accommodations driving U.S. innovation that are less prevalent in other world regions. European and Asian managers and institutions tend to be traditional, cautious, resistant to change, advocates of central planning (as opposed to entrepreneurial), and avoiders of risk. Free trade does not appeal to all businesspeople, particularly those who have endured years of recession. However, openness is vital to making the necessary changes to convert to the new economy, as companies will change only in the face of competition.

There has been some progress toward a global capitalism, as evidenced by merger and acquisition activity and by the conversion to the euro as a European regional currency. However, global productivity has not accelerated, spending on information technology is considerably less abroad than in the U.S., there is an ongoing shortage of skilled workers, and the euro is off more than 20% against the much stronger U.S. dollar compared to its value when trading began in 1999. The centers of developing new economy enterprise will include selected areas in Western Europe and Asia; see Exhibit 2-2.

Managing in the New Economy

Businesses held together by physical assets in the old economy may find them a burden in the new economy, and they are increasingly choosing to outsource or partner activities that are not essential or core competencies. This is an interesting turnaround from the integrated manufacturing enterprise of a century ago, when companies like Ford Motor chose to own the raw materials, control the conversion to finished goods, manage the distribution process to the ultimate consumer, and ally with suppliers like Firestone Tire and Rubber to ensure a constant flow of quality components.

Exhibit 2-2. Global centers of new economy activity.

Western Europe	
Ireland	Software, information processing
Central and Southern England	Financial information, Internet companies, biotechnology, software
Paris	Venture capital, biotechnology
Southern France	Telecommunications, electronics and microelectronics, biotechnology, aerospace research
Spain	Software, Internet companies
Belgium	Software
The Netherlands	Internet companies, venture capital
Germany	Software, biotechnology, venture capital
Scandinavia	Audio and cell telephone technology, scientific research
Asia	
Japan	Information technology
South Korea	Cell telephone technology
Taiwan	Computers and computer components
India	Software

Source: Reprinted from "Special Report: The New Economy," *Business Week,* January 31, 2000, pp. 73–92, by special permission, copyright © 2000 by The McGraw-Hill Companies, Inc. Various other business news sources were also researched.

New Economy Organizational Structure

Management provides an essential structure to a collection of people, resources, and information that would otherwise exist in anarchy or chaos. Whether or not the structure is ideal, it is an attempt at a configuration that will support corporate requirements and goals. Adjustments have been made over the years to adjust the concept to provide greater flexibility, permit decentralized decision-making, and reduce the command element of bureaucratic structures.

Old economy companies depend on hierarchical structures to manage, most often in the form of a line-and-staff organization. Such old economy structures exist for the control of resources and information, with middle managers functioning primarily to analyze results versus plans and to recount progress. This requires a more-or-less fixed set of information channels, reporting relationships and position responsibilities.

The old economy's authoritarian management ("do it or you're fired") has been replaced by the new economy's participative management ("let's all figure out how to get this project completed"). Authority works in an environment where we produce things because there is usually one best way to manufacture and sell.[9] Participation is more effective in companies that depend on intellectual capital, as communicated through computer networks, electronic mail ("e-mail"), and work teams, and there is less need for supervision.

Performance is based on results, not work form or content. The new economy organization will be fluid and dynamic and may require new organizational forms that will be strange and uncomfortable for today's managers. One likely outcome is fewer middle managers and a flatter span of control as the stability of the internal structure, markets, products, vendors, and customers disappears.

New Economy Accounting

Questionable accounting practices of the old economy are even more troublesome in the new economy as Internet companies without a history of earnings attempt to show attractive revenue growth. Recent Securities and Exchange Commission investigations have disclosed various practices intended to improve the appearance of financial statements when there are no earnings to report. Examples of these practices include:[10]

- Recognizing gross (vs. net) revenue (e.g., a travel agent's booking of the price of a ticket rather than the commission portion)

9. This is the basis of the scientific management movement as formulated by Frederick W. Taylor after World War I.
10. Reported in Catherine Yang, "Earth to Dot-Com Accountants," *Business Week*, April 3, 2000, pp. 40–41.

- Booking of sales prior to the occurrence of a transaction (e.g., recognizing software upgrade revenue prior to the sale)
- Assigning costs to sales, rather than to the cost of goods sold to improve reported gross margin results
- Intercompany bartering of Website advertising to inflate revenues, without any actual transfer of cash

These practices mislead investors, lenders, and customers as to the true volume of new economy business activity, and may hide profitability and other problems.

New Economy Values

Old economy companies defined values by the manufacturing and marketing of products. We used to justify the existence of the corporation as the repository of the critical mass of capital to convert raw materials to finished goods. Values could be thought of as:

- Land
- Labor
- Capital
- Innovation

New economy companies will define values by the process of thought. We use the corporate structure to create value from intangibles in various forms:[11]

- Design creativity
- Software architecture
- Management information
- Product and service innovations
- Human capital
- Scientific discovery
- Marketing expertise
- Customer and vendor relationships
- Internal culture
- Alliances and partnerships

11. This list was expanded from material in Joseph B. White, "Corporations Aren't Going to Disappear," special "Amazing Future" issue of *The Wall Street Journal*, January 1, 2000, pp. R36, R41.

Challenges of "Real-Time" Connectivity

The old rules we discussed in Chapter 1 for each discrete activity of the business timeline prior to, during, and after a transaction apply to corporations that emphasize production activities. The new rules have yet to be written but certainly do not involve methodical procedures developed over decades of trial-and-error progress. Old economy mistakes that resulted in marginal profits or losses were absorbed in the grand scheme of the industrial corporation for the development of an iterative knowledge base and to develop managers. In the new economy, there is little time for a repetitive learning experience, because the competition can use a failure to seize market share.

Connectivity and Business Relationships

The principal new economy attribute is the rapid dissemination of information throughout the business timeline, involving all of the parties to a transaction activity. The constituents of any commercial enterprise include itself, suppliers, customers, shareholders, and the public (usually represented by government). Internet e-commerce allows these parties to communicate on a nearly real-time basis to propose, consider, and execute business transactions, which in the past required time, deliberation, and research into past successes and failures.

As this occurs, the old linkages between a business and its constituents inevitably will change, with established relationships potentially weakened through the involvement of many more, previously unknown participants. Connectivity allows General Motors to buy from the same vendors in Michigan and Indiana that it has used for decades, but it also allows companies in Thailand and Singapore to bid for contracts, often at substantially lower labor rates.

Established affiliations were often based on long-time friendships with counterparties,[12] geographic proximity, or an established reputation for quality or service. These long-time business associ-

12. A "counterparty" is the opposite side of a transaction, that is, a seller is the counterparty of a buyer.

ates will see their competitive roles deteriorate and their investment in such preferred positions become nearly worthless.

This is not a trivial matter, because business has been conducted for many decades on the basis of corporate relationship, personal friendship, entertainment, and general social interaction. While old economy companies would probably like to continue to do business in that manner, they cannot, because of the necessity to become as efficient as possible. Connectivity in the new economy will force this situation, and businesses will either become competitively ruthless or decline.

Connectivity and Decision-Making

The special challenge of the new economy is that corporate actions and decisions no longer can be discrete, specialized job functions reached in isolated offices or plant locations. Organizations become a continuum of actions, most of which occur without significant delays and the requirement for system and personnel interfaces. Here are two examples:

- Securities dealers have expedited the settlement of investment transactions through global standardization and systemic reductions in clearing times.[13] Further technological changes will electronically link market participants, eliminating auction markets and transaction costs.[14]
- EDI (electronic data interchange) standards developed through the American National Standards Institute (the ANSI X-12 committee) allow companies to communicate electronically to place orders and to invoice and authorize payments.[15]

13. See the Group of 30 Website, www.group30.org. and its various publications, e.g., *Clearance and Settlement Systems Status Report*, 1992.
14. The Pacific Stock Exchange is scheduled to convert to automated trading in the fall of 2000, through the electronic communication network (ECN), Archipelago. See Neil Weinberg, "Fear, Greed and Technology," *Forbes*, May 15, 2000, pp. 170–176.
15. See the Data Interchange Standards Association Website, www.disa.org. An important published reference on electronic data interchange is Thomas P. Colberg, ed., *The Price Waterhouse EDI Handbook* (New York: John Wiley & Sons, 1995).

Connectivity and Intermediaries

The old economy supports institutions that provide essential intermediary services based on expertise and relationship. Any business function that stands between a producer and the ultimate user is providing information and access to markets for profit, realized either as a percentage of the sale or as a transaction fee. Examples include insurance brokers and agents, manufacturers' representatives, real estate agents, wholesalers, and pharmaceutical detail personnel (who explain new medicines to physicians and other medical professionals).

Connectivity allows these old economy closed, proprietary data networks to evolve into new economy open, accessible information exchanges. The informational and access functions performed by intermediaries may not have a role in the new economy. On-line communication will eliminate their special roles and disseminate their knowledge to any interested party. The Internet can provide complete dissemination of information regarding products and prices to any interested buyer or seller. If this occurs, the layers of cost that reflect relationship or intermediary functions may become insupportable.

Transaction Connectivity

Some commentators believe that the connectivity potential of the Internet will match its potential for changing the way we provide and use capital, forcing greater efficiencies onto the private sector through lower financial costs.[16] Apparently, if this does occur, the traditional providers of intermediation services, such as commercial and investment bankers, will decline in significance. However, a close read of predicted Internet activities focuses on the retail customer, citing such benefits as a 100:1 cost advantage over the expense of doing business through a branch teller and a 25:1 advantage for ATM transactions. Similar advantages are cited for mortgage loan origination and investing.

"Experts" have made few sweeping conclusions on the implica-

16. See, for example, "The Internet Age: All the World's an Auction Now," *Business Week*, October 4, 1999, pp. 120–128.

tions for business finance. It seems unlikely that borrowers and lenders/investors will somehow mate through magical Internet connections or that capital will find investment opportunities by clicking onto Websites. Participation in capital markets is a highly technical financial function that is unlikely to be easily converted to the Internet.

Connecting Buyers and Sellers

Many old economy sellers reside in industries approaching oligopoly, where there are a limited number of sellers and any participant can influence the market price and quantity offered. The Commerce Department calculates that 32% of U.S. industries (146 of 457) experience two-thirds of their industry value-added by eight or fewer companies, a measurement of industry concentration.[17] Some 16 of 42 industries (or 38%) were industries where the value of shipped products exceeded $10 billion and the concentration ratios were more than 40% (excluding highly technological products and perishables such as processed foods). See the chapter appendix for more complete data.

These selling firms are typically larger than their buyers, which gives them the leverage to influence the purchase decision through marketing and advertising activities. Important seller advantages result through control of the counterparty relationship. Inefficiencies provide inherent advantages to established companies, including opportunities for cross-selling, the control of busy channels of distribution, the ownership of strong brands, and loyal customers.[18]

These competitive advantages almost certainly disappear in the new economy. The largest fungible-product, concentrated industries are very susceptible to the competition in a global e-commerce environment, particularly forest and paper products, chemicals, petroleum products, and metals. The leading companies in these industries enjoy oligopolistic profits compared to their smaller competitors, 50% greater measured by returns-on-sales (ROS) and 40% greater measured by return-on-equity (ROE); see Exhibit 2-3. Similar results are attained in other industries.

17. Extracted by data reported by SIC code classification; "Concentration Ratios in Manufacturing," *U.S. Census of Manufactures*, 1992, Table MC92-S-2. This is the last year for which data are available.
18. Evans and Wurster, *Blown to Bits*, p. 106.

Exhibit 2-3. Oligopolistic profitability measures in selected U.S. industries.

Company Ranking Within Industry	Forest/ Paper Products		Chemicals		Petroleum		Metals/ Metal Products	
	ROS	ROE	ROS	ROE	ROS	ROE	ROS	ROE
No. 1	1	2	28	60	5	12	13	41
No. 2	4	19	7	16	3	10	9	17
No. 3	13	33	6	11	6	12	2	6
No. 4	4	7	7	18	3	10	1	4
No. 5	2	9	5	11	4	16	9	18
No. 6	7	46	5	7	3	21	6	17
No. 7	3	12	9	15	4	13	3	6
No. 8	4	7	6	18	11	16	2	5
8 Co. Average	4.8	16.8	9.1	19.5	4.8	13.8	5.4	13.6
Industry Median	4	9	6	15	3	12	3	10

Calculated eight-company average compared to industry median:
ROS (return-on-sales) = +53.1%.
ROE (return-on-equity) = +40.8%.
Source: Extracted from Fortune 500 issue of *Fortune Magazine*, April 17, 2000.

Market concentration will inevitably decline as smaller U.S. and international competitors use the Internet to sell at prices and on delivery terms that are superior to those offered by these large U.S. companies.

At the present time the popular search engines[19] cannot differentiate among sellers' wares to determine which meet buyers' requirements. With innovation in search technology, searches will be based on standards and structure, producing perhaps several dozen viable sellers that can be solicited for bids. Buyers can also solicit sellers through the Internet using existing purchasing protocols. The big change will be the process through which vendors are sought, as the universe of potential sellers is increasingly unrestricted to particular locations or regions.

When this starts to occur, the old relationships between buyers and sellers will become obsolete, and buyers will be able to go anywhere in search of the best offer. The best offer will inevitably mean lower costs, higher quality, and product features that are optimal for the needs of the deal. Costs will be squeezed, as will the profits enjoyed in the old economy.

The Timeline and Connectivity

The most significant impact of connectivity will be to force corporations to re-examine the interrelationship of cashflow timeline elements.[20] The old economy supports the existence of discrete activities along the timeline as each manager decides thoughtfully and deliberately how to proceed with each business decision. Let's see how the timeline might work in the old and the new economies.

In the old economy, a typical sales cycle is completed when an order is placed and accepted by the selling company. Negotiations have resolved pricing discounts, marketing allowances, extended payment terms, and other special requirements, but these negotiations may have taken up to two weeks. Products are manufactured and shipped over a cycle lasting two months and invoiced during a

19. Search engines are guides to Internet Websites that seek out sites on the basis of specific inquiry criteria selected by the user. Prominent search engines include Yahoo and Excite.
20. See Chapter 1, pp. 21–22.

one week period, with payment expected in one month. A check is finally received after one and one-half months and deposited and cleared after another week. The entire inflow cycle requires five months, with stops and starts at each step along the way.

The Integrated Timeline

In the new economy, the concept of discrete business functions will give way to continuous activities. The sales cycle will be compressed to a few days, with requests for bids, bidding, and counteroffers all occurring during sessions at the computer. We'll assume that the manufacturing and delivery cycle requires the same two months, although there is significant potential for reducing the entire raw materials order cycle through "just-in-time" e-commerce.[21] Although notification of shipment and invoicing will be done on-line, payment still requires one and one-half months. However, the electronic funds transfer mechanism (the ACH) used by the buyer will be completed next-day.[22] The new economy cycle will require some three and one-half months, and this time is devoted to manufacturing and to collecting funds from the buyer.

Connectivity changes the entire timeline interrelationship and eliminates every old economy delay except for those beyond the reach of electronic commerce. The savings of about one and one-half months (or 25–30%!) in this sales/collection cycle (and in its mirror image, the payables/disbursement cycle) affects the positions of both the seller and the buyer. The seller is affected as:

21. There are several excellent references on "just-in-time" and manufacturing resource planning. See, e.g., John E. Schorr, *Purchasing in the 21st Century: A Guide to State-of-the-Art Techniques and Strategies* (2nd ed.) (New York: John Wiley & Sons, 1998).
22. Electronic funds transfer mechanisms include clearings on a same-day basis (Fedwire) and next-day basis (ACH and EDI). ACH (Automated Clearing House) transactions are batch processed, stored, and forwarded, with files sent to banks by initiating organizations and transmitted electronically to the receiving bank for credit to the vendor or other payee. As the amount of data that can accompany an ACH is limited, other formats with larger data fields have become available, and these are generically known as EDI (electronic data interchange). The Fedwire system is operated by the Federal Reserve System, with payment initiated and received by banks on a same-day, final basis, that is, a payment sent cannot generally be recovered. A Fedwire costs about 100 times the price of an ACH.

- The costs and efforts of sale are largely eliminated with the requests for bids, bidding, and negotiation completed on-line.
- The receivables cycle is altered because the presentation of the invoice is also on-line, rather than through a paper-based document.

The buyer is affected as :

- The search for vendors is extended and simplified by electronic requests for bidding and the completion of the selection process.
- The matching of invoice and payables data can be accomplished through electronic feeds of data from the vendor to the buyer's accounting ledger.

Both parties are affected as:

- The requirement for real-time decision-making in accepting/ modifying/rejecting a business opportunity changes standard profitability assumptions.
- The 25–30% reduction in the times required for the sales/collection cycle (or the payables/disbursement cycle) will be a joint good, with the specific assignment of benefits subject to a negotiation between the parties.

In the balance of Part I we present specific concepts for managing in the new, e-commerce economy. Chapter 3 examines procedures for constructing financial metrics for e-commerce, and Chapters 4 and 5 describe a specific company situation that uses these procedures.

Chapter 2 Appendix

ECONOMIC CONCENTRATION

The following data show the concentration percentage for the eight largest companies in industries with greater than $10 billion in value-added shipments. "Concentration" is a measure of oligopolistic control of an industry by a limited number of sellers, which may lead to such uncompetitive behaviors as high pricing and limited product innovation. "Special Circumstances" indicate industries that are not immediate candidates for extensive e-commerce competition because of the requirement for rapid delivery or thorough knowledge of local tastes ("Perishable") or extensive technological expertise in product design and manufacture ("High Tech [Technology]").

Dept. of Commerce SIC Code	Industry	Shipments ($MM)	% value added by 8 largest companies	Special circumstances
2015	Poultry & egg processing	$ 23,845	45	Perishable
2022	Cheese, natural & processed	$ 18,344	60	Perishable
2026	Fluid milk	$ 21,921	30	Perishable
2033	Canned fruits & vegetables	$ 15,071	42	Perishable
2048	Prepared foods	$ 14,378	33	Perishable
2051	Bread/cake/related products	$ 18,143	49	Perishable
2064	Candy & confectionaries	$ 10,207	59	Perishable
2075	Soybean oil mills	$ 10,651	91	Perishable
2082	Malt beverages	$ 17,340	98	Perishable
2086	Bottled/canned soft drinks	$ 25,423	48	Perishable
2111	Cigarettes	$ 29,746	94	Perishable
2411	Logging	$ 13,879	26	
2421	Sawmills	$ 21,065	20	

Dept. of Commerce SIC Code	Industry	Shipments ($MM)	% value added by 8 largest companies	Special circumstances
2621	Paper mills	$ 32,786	49	
2631	Paperboard mills	$ 16,140	52	
2653	Fiber boxes	$ 19,790	45	
2676	Sanitary paper products	$ 15,623	82	
2711	Newspapers	$ 33,880	37	Perishable
2721	Periodical publishing	$ 22,075	31	Perishable
2731	Book publishing	$ 16,753	38	Perishable
2741	Misc. publishing	$ 10,977	44	Perishable
2819	Industrial inorganic chemicals	$ 18,171	50	
2821	Plastics materials/resins	$ 31,557	39	
2824	Man-made organic fibers	$ 11,115	90	
2834	Pharmaceutical preparations	$ 50,413	42	
2841	Soap, other detergents	$ 14,762	77	Perishable
2844	Toilet preparations	$ 18,753	55	Perishable
2851	Paints & allied products	$ 14,960	43	
2911	Petroleum refining	$136,579	49	
3011	Tires & inner tubes	$ 11,810	91	
3081	Plastics film & sheet	$ 10,643	27	
3089	Plastic products	$ 45,528	8	
3273	Ready-mixed concrete	$ 12,013	11	
3312	Blast furnaces/steel mills	$ 16,565	58	
3353	Aluminum	$ 10,693	86	
3357	Nonferrous metals	$ 13,035	43	
3411	Metal cans	$ 12,112	74	
3444	Sheet metal work	$ 11,486	13	
3465	Automotive stampings	$ 15,821	56	
3519	Internal combustion engines	$ 11,824	75	
3531	Construction machinery	$ 13,485	53	
3559	Special industrial machinery	$ 11,379	18	
3571	Electronic computers	$ 38,206	59	High Tech
3577	Computer peripherals	$ 12,157	56	High Tech
3599	Machinery except electrical	$ 19,085	2	High Tech
3661	Telephone/telegraph equipment	$ 12,465	61	High Tech
3663	Radio & TV equipment	$ 19,463	53	High Tech
3674	Semiconductors	$ 32,144	58	High Tech
3679	Electronic components	$ 23,749	35	High Tech
3711	Motor vehicles	$151,712	91	
3714	Motor vehicle parts	$ 75,034	57	
3721	Aircraft	$ 62,938	93	High Tech
3724	Aircraft engines	$ 22,398	84	High Tech
3728	Aircraft parts	$ 19,458	62	High Tech

Dept. of Commerce SIC Code	Industry	Shipments ($MM)	% value added by 8 largest companies	Special circumstances
3731	Ship building & repairing	$ 10,609	67	High Tech
3761	Guided missiles & space vehicles	$ 19,423	93	High Tech
3812	Aeronautical/nautical	$ 35,215	48	High Tech
3841	Surgical/medical instruments	$ 13,366	37	High Tech
3842	Surgical supplies	$ 13,801	31	High Tech
3861	Photographic equipment	$ 22,121	83	High Tech

Source: Extracted from data reported by 457 manufacturing sector Standard Industrial Classification (SIC) code classifications, in U.S. Department of Commerce, ''Concentration Ratios in Manufacturing,'' 1992 *U.S. Census of Manufactures* Table MC92-S-2.

Chapter 3

New Economy Financial Metrics

Labor is prior to, and independent of, capital. . . . Capital has its rights, which are as worthy of protection as any other rights.

—Abraham Lincoln (1809–1865),
First Annual Message to Congress

The workhorse part of corporate finance in the new economy will not be mergers and acquisitions, or commercial or investment banking, or treasury management. Instead, it will be the specialty of "transaction finance," the discipline of financial decision-making for the sale of a business product or service. In this chapter we discuss problems with old economy financial metrics and the changes necessary to provide meaningful profitability measures in the new economy to protect the capital of the corporation.

Old Economy Transactions

A business deal results from the interaction of the sales and marketing efforts of a selling company with the buying company, reinforced by a history of quality products and services, superior customer support, and access to senior management. The buying company provides purchasing expertise, specific product requirements, target price ceilings, and delivery times. In addition, there are numerous other variables particular to every business relationship.

Old Economy Relationships

The weighting or importance of the variables that influence the selling and buying behavior of companies is specific to each counterparty situation and ripens over years of association, bickering, friendship, and trust. A business relationship in many ways is like a family situation, and, once established, it may continue indefinitely unless the parties become estranged (i.e., divorced) due to unresolved conflict. In the old economy it is unusual for a manager to sever a corporate contact unless service or quality has seriously deteriorated, pricing becomes uncompetitive, the buying company's credit-worthiness becomes suspect, or other serious problems arise.

Old economy companies experience instances of inferior performance, but they usually adjust to eventually achieve targeted ROS or ROE. A mediocre result may stem from a special accommodation for a loyal customer, an error in estimating costs or production time, a pricing discount to win business, adverse weather conditions, a misunderstanding of design or engineering requirements, quality control, or any of numerous other causes. An occasional failure does not usually doom a business relationship.

Long-time counterparties help each other to whatever extent they can, because of friendship but also because neither party benefits from the economic loss of the other. Buying companies depend on strong, reliable sellers; vendors obviously need someone to buy their products and services. In addition, changing supply sources require a search for qualified vendors, a review of their credentials and qualifications, and other efforts at due diligence. Finding new customers requires extensive sales and marketing efforts.

Old Economy Accounting

To a significant extent, business managers muddle through[1] on the basis of financial "information" that uses account codes and descriptions with little relevance to twenty-first-century issues. It has long been acknowledged that economic and accounting treatment of assets and expenses can be quite different. We discussed the essential importance of intellectual capital in Chapter 2, yet we are not permitted to account for this most important resource on the balance sheet.

The economic value of human resources to high technology businesses is unmistakable.[2] The stock market recognizes the value

1. As described in Chapter 1, pp. 22–23.
2. There is a growing body of work on human or intellectual capital. See, for example, Thomas O. Davenport, *Human Capital: What It Is and Why People Invest It* (San Francisco: Jossey-Bass Publishers, 1999); and Thomas A. Stewart, *Intellectual Capital: The New Wealth of Organizations* (New York: Doubleday, 1997). A recent article discusses the business of

of people, as industries with high market price-earnings (P/E) ratios, such as biotechnology, publishing, image types of consumer products (e.g., cosmetics), computers, and pharmaceuticals, are those with creative or scientific products and services. Industries with low valuations, including manufacturing, banking, public utilities, and construction, are oriented toward repetitive processes. See Exhibit 3-1.

The human capital issue is one of several problems in developing useful old economy financial data. Some others are briefly noted.

• *Accounting Rules.* Data are presented on the basis of accounting rules, rather than of "real world" considerations. For example, the life of a machine for accounting depreciation may be eight years, but the actual useful life may be 12 years if the machine is properly maintained and run on a one-shift operation, or six years if new equipment is installed.

• *Averaging.* Data are lumped together by accounting code without regard for functional analysis or specific transactions. For example, banking fees are reported together (and may not even be properly identified if payment is by balance compensation[3]), as are warehousing fees and charges for most supplies and materials.

• *Avoidable Costs.* Accounting data are difficult to interpret because certain costs may not be avoidable. For example, space may be properly allocated to an operation at $20 per square foot. However, there may not be an alternative use for that space should the operation be outsourced or eliminated. In this situation, should the space be included in an analysis? Management supervision, some labor costs, and computer time charges present similar dilemmas.

• *Relevance.* Although cost accounting attempts to provide specific expense data on production activities, the data provide little

---

licensing such intellectual assets as patents, copyrights, and business practices: Carol O. Madigan, "Capitalizing on Intellectual Capital," *Business Finance*, May 2000, pp. 79–86.

3. "Balance compensation" involves the payment for bank services by balances left on deposit with the bank rather than by direct fee charges. A credit balance is translated to a fee equivalent by the application of a short-term interest rate, usually the prevailing 91-day U.S. Treasury bill rate.

flexibility for the consideration of various manufacturing strategies. For example, not much support is provided if we wish to evaluate outsourcing, a change in production scheduling, or an alternative plant site.

Activity-Based Costing

Various developments attempt to overcome the problems of old economy accounting, to improve the alignment of financial and accounting data, and to enhance the accuracy of product costing. Activity-based costing (ABC) analyzes all organizational activities to support decision-making by re-configuring the general ledger into business activities. (In contrast, recall that traditional accounting bases reporting on such general ledger categories as wages, supplies, and cash.) ABC is concerned primarily with identifying and analyzing indirect activities. Indirect charges are investigated to discover the activities that cause or "drive" these costs.

Exhibit 3-1. Price-earnings ratios of selected old and new industries.

Old Economy	
Aerospace and defense	19
Aluminum and steel	24
Banks	13
Coal, oil, and gas	23
Machine and hand tools	11
New Economy	
Computer software	72
Drugs and research	43
Electronic instruments	61
Entertainment	76
Telecommunications equipment/services	50
All-industry composite	29

Source: Reprinted from *Business Week* Corporate Scoreboard, 1st Quarter 2000, May 15, 2000, pp. 111–142, by special permission, copyright © 2000 by The McGraw-Hill Companies, Inc.

Examples of "cost-drivers" include the number of production batches, the number of purchase orders, the number of suppliers, the number of engineering changes, and the number of manufacturing steps or setups. These activities are the critical factors that drive expenses, as applied to individual products, types of business, or customers. This cost-driver determination is critical to ABC, since standard cost accounting uses meaningless aggregated volumes, such as product volume, worker man-hours, and square footage.

Activities in a manufacturing environment can include processing batches, inspecting finished goods, and packaging for shipment; in a bank, authorizing credit facilities, opening loan accounts, and monitoring loan repayments. Exhibit 3-2 lists illustrative timeline activities and cost-drivers that may be encountered in attempting an analysis of the manufacturing and customer/sales cycles reviewed in Part II of this book. The focus is on *why* costs are incurred, not merely *how much*.

An ABC effort requires that activities are defined organization-wide; otherwise, different definitions may be used in various business units, making comparisons meaningless. Cost-drivers can be identified from these activities and often relate to volumes, quality, time, and service levels. Data gathering efforts follow, usually focusing on financial accounts; transaction processing systems; the general ledger and supporting, detailed ledgers (such as the cash ledger); and customer information files.

ABC has been particularly useful in assigning costs to products and services previously bundled and sold as a package. For example, bankers have historically offered credit and non-credit services to corporate customers without separating relevant costs by product or by market served. Lines of credit are made available for a fraction of a percentage point; labor-intensive cash management products (e.g., wholesale lockboxes, to be discussed in Chapter 9) are sold for about 50 cents apiece. ABC determines the precise cost structure of each unbundled product, allowing more rational pricing (or providing a rationale for a decision to leave the market to the other bankers).[4]

4. Two good ABC references are James A. Brimson, *Activity Accounting, an Activity-Based Costing Approach* (New York: John Wiley & Sons, 1991) and Gary Cokins, *Activity-Based Cost Management* (New York: McGraw-Hill, 1996).

Exhibit 3-2. Illustrative ABC activities and cost-drivers.

Activity	*Cost-Driver*
Product-Related	
Materials Purchasing	No. of purchase orders
	No. of line items per purchase order
Manufacturing (work-in-process)	No. of work orders
	No. of machine hours by product
	No. of inspections
	No. of reworks
Invoicing	No. of invoices
	No. of statements
Receipt of Good Funds	No. of checks received
	No. of bank deposits
Customer- or Sales-Related	
Selling	No. of customers
	No. of sales calls
	No. of orders
Order Completion	No. of items picked from inventory
	No. of order changes
	No. of complaints

Financial Limitations

In addition to accounting limitations, there are significant financial constraints on "old economy-type analysis": relevance and the time value of money.

• *Relevance.* Events being analyzed are occurring now or will occur in the future. There may only be a marginal relationship to costs for equivalent transactions that were experienced in the past.

For example, we may analyze a new product on the basis of the costs incurred in manufacturing and marketing its predecessor products. However, past labor costs may be significantly different due to various factors, including:

- A change in the production location that affects labor costs
- The acquisition of technology that automates the manufacturing process
- New plant layout that makes the entire process more efficient
- Just-in-time inventory management that requires more highly skilled workers to operate

Similarly, there may be variations in materials, overhead, and other costs. Many factors can change in the planning horizon for business transactions that may substantively affect the calculation of meaningful budgets and plans. Part II of this book provides a detailed discussion of each of these cost elements and their relationship to a financial measurement process.

   • *Time Value of Money.* Traditional financial data do not account in any manner for the time value of money. A monetary unit (i.e., a dollar) is received or spent at some point during a fiscal period, usually a year. However, in calculating the return from that transaction, there is no consideration of the specific timing of that activity during that interval. Here's a simple example of a sale of product from inventory:

Purchase of raw materials:	January 15
Manufacture and assembly of product:	February 1
Sale of product:	March 1
Issue invoice:	March 15
Payment due date:	April 1
Actual payment date:	April 15

The period from January 15 to April 15—three months—is a typical transaction cycle in business. It is a long, expensive cycle if we ignore the likely cost of capital of 12–16% (as we discussed in Chapter 1), and it can easily turn a planned profit into a loss. This topic is explored more fully in the Appendix to Chapter 3.

New Economy Transactions

Despite ABC and other refinements in accounting and information systems, corporations are unprepared for decision-making in an e-commerce environment. Only a handful of organizations have considered the hundreds of price and cost elements and sub-elements in their various businesses and can anticipate the impact of a change in one or more of these elements on profitability.

We've accepted this deficiency in the old economy as a cost of doing business. We have not encountered this in the retail sector (i.e., business-to-consumer sales), the primary focus of early Internet activity, because retail prices and service are not generally subject to discussion, bidding, and negotiation.[5] But in business-to-business e-commerce, this is a recipe for disaster because:

> ***You will be making rapid response commitments to counterparties you may hardly know.***

E-commerce has been touted as a "positive-sum" game, where all parties gain and there are no losers (except those who don't participate). This can be true, but only in the long run when companies become sufficiently knowledgeable about their businesses to compete and survive. If you make uninformed decisions (or pass on an e-commerce opportunity), you may experience substantial losses. You can reduce transaction costs by using e-commerce, but only if you have superior information on internal processes and on your customer.

Transaction Finance Defined

The old economy income statement system of financial planning and analysis has no meaning in an e-commerce environment. Instead, the new approach will be transaction finance. The structure of a transaction may include special pricing, credit and payment arrangements, quality guarantees, sales rebates or other assistance, or nearly any conceivable manufacturing or marketing accommoda-

---

5. Except for eBay, Priceline.com, and other Internet retail auction services.

tion. E-commerce requires the capacity to track data on customers (or vendors) and review the facts of a proposed exchange, including all of the special arrangements requested by the buyer that constitute exceptions to the "standard" deal.

While e-commerce decision-making may not require an immediate response capability, there will be pressure for a prompt reaction to requests for business commitments or declinations. The finance function will be expected to support the financial requirements of vendors and customers, to analyze the likely profitability of each business opportunity, and to provide negotiating support to optimize the company's bargaining position. This is a significant change from old economy practice, which permitted time to reflect on each deal, to consult with colleagues, and to review past successes and failures.

Transaction finance will be used to analyze the nearly real-time completion of financial arrangements for an e-commerce sale. Functions will include negotiating credit, assisting with payment arrangements, negotiating with trading partners, determining whether a product can be manufactured to meet the buyer's expectation of performance and price, and handling various other manufacturing, marketing, and administrative issues.

At the present time there is no established functional expertise that provides these essential activities, with the tasks of transaction finance variously assigned to accounting, sales, credit, or other areas. The financial manager best understands how these variables can affect the target return because of his or her knowledge of the time value of money.

Transaction Finance Work-Days

To overcome the deficiencies of old transaction data, it is necessary to calculate the work-day equivalent of any transaction and to convert those days to a profit margin impact factor. The concept of a "work-day" allows the implicit recognition of the time value of money, while forcing attention to the length of time necessary to complete each significant work task. In other words, by focusing on work-days, we better understand the actual time to complete a business activity, be it purchasing materials, manufacturing products, holding goods in inventory until sale, or awaiting payment once invoices have been sent to buyers.

Work-days are the number of days to accomplish each series of tasks required to complete a set of business functions. To manufacture and distribute a product in e-business may require 50 work-days. Each task in that effort can be calculated as a work-day equivalent. Once a work-day standard is established, changes in the ROS and ROE can be calculated from the details of a particular transaction. Each change to a set of business functions can be restated as positive or negative days against the standard. If the target of 50 days becomes 60 days, the target returns may be expected to decline by 20% (60–50 days). We can then decide if we want to accept, negotiate a change, or reject the transaction.

If our target net return on sales (ROS) on the manufacture and distribution of a product is 10%, we must establish precise work-day rules for attaining that target. Work-day rules "track" the rules we have used in the old economy but will be explicit; they will be stated and quantified and controlling; that is, they can be ignored but only at the manager's (and the business's) peril. Work-day rules will drive how much we can spend on marketing; on each step of the production process, including ordering raw materials, paying labor and carrying inventory; and on invoicing and collecting.

Now what happens to our target return if there are deviations from these work-day rules, if, for example:

- The materials we purchased are imperfect or are held in inventory for long periods of time.
- Any of the manufacturing components are delayed.
- We help finance the customer's credit.
- Customers take longer to order or to pay.

The Automobile Parts Supplier

Let's consider the example of an automobile parts supplier.[6] This company plans to provide castings for light trucks and sport-utility vehicles by working a normal eight-hour shift with two to three hours of overtime, as needed. The ROS is expected to be 5%, resulting in an ROE of 16%. However, consumer demand for these types

6. The following example is developed from an actual situation described in "Just-in-Time Manufacturing Is Working Overtime," *Business Week,* November 8, 1999, pp. 36–37.

of vehicles has overwhelmed the company with parts orders, forcing it to operate 24 hours a day. Overtime, repairs, and charges for freight have increased manufacturing costs, causing the ROS to fall to $3\frac{1}{2}\%$, with the actual ROE down to 12%.

Could the auto parts company have anticipated the problem? The customer of the auto parts supplier, an automobile manufacturer, did not foresee the demand and, with its own reduced workforces and just-in-time inventory systems, allowed the burden to fall on their suppliers. This permits the auto manufacturer to be globally competitive but places a new and perhaps unmanageable imposition on their suppliers, who may not be able to respond. In this situation, the problem resides in one portion of a company's timeline—the segment relating to manufacturing—leading to higher costs of production, as well as to slower product delivery and lower profits.

In any business there are quite possibly hundreds of financial and process metric elements in any decision-making process. Exhibit 3-3 includes 25 selected elements for a typical manufacturing or service company. We discuss financial metrics in the remainder of Part I of the book, and the process throughout Part II.

The Widget Deal

In an e-commerce/new economy world, your company will be making decisions on all of these factors as business opportunities occur. How would transaction finance work in an actual situation?

What Your Customer Wants

Let's assume that your customer is ready to buy 200 gross widgets but wants a 4% price discount, guaranteed delivery to particular quality standards, billing no earlier than 30 days after delivery, and an advertising rebate to help with sales costs.

This customer typically pays you by a two-day check 50 days after being invoiced. Can you sell the widgets under these terms and still make your target return of $100/widget (20%)? In the old economy you had weeks to decide. In the new economy, driven by e-commerce, you may have only minutes to decide. Does your financial system give you the answer? Not likely.

Exhibit 3-3. Process metric elements.

Materials Purchases

1. Timing of materials purchases
2. Price discounts offered
3. Commodity analysis and hedging
4. Accounts payable
5. Freight/other physical movement

Work-in-Process

6. Setup of manufacturing activities
7. Inspection of work-in-process
8. Scrap, spoilage and re-work
9. Payroll

Invoice Preparation

10. Assembly of data from work areas
11. Data verification and keying
12. Matching of draft invoices against file documents
13. Mailing of invoices and collection mail time

Receipt of Good Funds

14. Timing of payment receipt vs. due date
15. Collection processing time
16. Collection availability time
17. Disputed/delayed customer payments

Sales, Marketing, and Finance

18. Sales and marketing
19. Credit reviews
20. Collection cycle time (days sales outstanding)
21. Cost of capital
22. Cost and extent of banking services

Service Industry Cost Elements

23. Billable and non-billable time management
24. Customer, geographic or service profitability
25. Volume of services provided

In doing the analysis, we determine that a target net margin of 20% would be reduced by one-sixth because of the various special requirements of your widget customer: the price discount, quality standards, the timing of your invoice, and the advertising rebate. In terms of work time or equivalents (in the case of such cost elements as materials and collection mail and availability), we plan a total of 120 days with break-even at 150 days. In other words, do we make our target return if the terms of the deal are changed? As we would require 140 days, we will be marginally profitable (a 2.7% return) on a ledger basis. We will be using the term *ledger* throughout this book to refer to the occurrence of a cash event without regard for the timing of the in- or outflow.

If we were using formal time value of money analysis, we would convert the result to the present value of the revenues (the inflows) and of costs (outflows) on the basis of known events pertinent to each customer, product, and process. Known characteristics of each customer include quality requirements and payment patterns; of products, sales rebates and pricing discounts; and of processes, recurring work-in-process delays and the invoicing cycle. What we typically do not know to the specific transaction are materials, direct labor, and overhead. (Over the next 10 years or so, all contributing elements will have real-time connections to a "return" model, including data on costs we are not typically tracking to individual manufacturing activities.)

What the Outcome Would Be

Look closely at Exhibit 3-4. It shows how a $200 target net margin per widget can actually turn into a *loss* when calculations consider the time value of money. It should be noted that the present value of expenses is a calculation that is based on the estimated timing of the cash outflow for each cost category, which will vary by element. For example, materials, payroll, and other expenses will be paid on various dates that would be included in the analysis. The projected margin on the original assumptions for the 200 gross widgets was $5.75 million; the ledger margin becomes $750,000; the actual *loss* is $200,000! The widget deal can be saved by negotiating better terms and/or improving internal processes. Otherwise, it should be declined.

Outcomes similar to the widget results happen frequently to

Exhibit 3-4. Transaction finance calculations (per widget) (present value calculated at 12%).

Revenue/ Cost Element	Target Work-Days*	Actual Work-Days*	% of Sales	Target $	Actual $	Present Value of $
Revenue (inflows)			100.0%	$1000	$960	$918
Expenses (outflow)			80.0%	$800	$933	$925
Materials	25	29	− 3.5%			
Work-in-process	20	22	− 1.7%			
Invoicing cycle	5	7	− 1.7%			
Receipt of funds	40	45	− 4.3%			
Sales/marketing	25	30	− 4.3%			
General and administrative	5	7	− 1.7%			
Net margin**	120	140	2.7%	$200	$27	($7)

*Equivalents.
**Based on target revenue.

companies that plan a reasonable profit, experience a "ledger" minimal profit, and actually sustain a loss when the time value of money is considered. Our clients report marginal results on important products and services, yet are unable to find the source of the shortfall. Intensive investigation consistently determines that there is no one source; rather, the cause is the interplay of various slippages in assumptions, performance, and results, as measured by the financial metrics.

We'll do a detailed review of a time value of money approach to financial metrics in the chapters that follow. Please note that we will not be calculating present value in developing these measurements, because present value does not explicitly disclose causes of delays and opportunities for efficiencies. Instead, we'll be using the cost of the imputed interest for the work-days required to complete the transaction, which takes us into the heart of transaction finance.

Chapter 3 Appendix

TIME VALUE OF MONEY FINANCE CONCEPTS

This chapter refers to the time value of money (TVM) as a factor in financial decision-making.

The Concept of TVM

TVM is the concept that a dollar (or other currency) earned or spent today has a greater worth than one earned or spent at a future time. The calculation of these amounts is based on an interest rate or factor that determines the equivalent future value on the basis of the amount of elapsed time. For example, $1 earned today is worth $1.06 in one year at an assumed rate of interest of 6% ($1 times [1.0 + .06]); $1 earned one year from now is worth 94.3 cents today ($1 divided by [1.0 + .06]).

This procedure is used in four types of TVM applications, all of which require the number of years or future time to be specified.

   • *Future (or Compound) Value: The Future Value of Today's Money.* What will a dollar invested today be worth in the future?

   • *Present Value: The Current Worth of a Future Sum.* What is a dollar worth today that is earned in the future?

   • *Future Sum of an Annuity: The Future Value of a Series of Payments of a Fixed Amount.* What will a dollar invested each year until retirement (or some other date in the future) be worth at that future time?

   • *Present Value of an Annuity: The Current Value of a Series of Payments of a Fixed Amount.* What amount would be equivalent today to a series of future payments, such as the principal and interest charges to retire a loan?

Calculating TVM

Tables and financial calculators are available for each application of TVM. You must provide two of three variables—the interest rate, the interest factor, and the number of years—in order to calculate the outcome. Most often the interest rate and the number of years are known, allowing you to determine the interest factor and the resulting TVM. For example, an interest rate of 10% and a time period of 10 years has a present value of .386. If we were to make an investment expecting $1,000 in 10 years at 10%, we would have a TVM "gain" if this venture required an investment of less than $386 now (the $1,000 times the interest factor, .386).

The interest rate used in these calculations is the cost of capital (discussed in Chapter 1), the cost of debt, and equity capital on our balance sheet. The number of years is the expected future time of an event, such as the years until the sale of a product or the maturity of a loan. In capital budgeting decisions, we generally assume the outflows of cash at year "0" and estimate the years and amounts of future cash inflows. We can then calculate cash in- and outflows at the same moment in time—today—using present value.

NPV and IRR

A project costing $1,000 today with various inflows in years 1–4 will have the following result (the net present value or "NPV") at an assumed interest rate of 10%:

Year	Cash flow	Interest factor	Present value
1	$500	.91	$455
2	$400	.83	$332
3	$300	.75	$225
4	$100	.68	$68
Total inflows			$1,080
Less outflow			− $1,000
Net present value			$80

This TVM calculation can also be stated as a measurement of the interest rate equivalent of the flows (the internal rate of return or "IRR"), that interest rate that equates the present value of the inflows to the outflows. Using these same assumptions, the calculated IRR is 15%. The rule is that when the IRR is greater than the cost of capital, the investment should be undertaken. As the IRR of 15% in our example exceeds the cost of capital of 10%, we would proceed.

These procedures assume knowledge about the expected timing of each cash event, which may not be realistic given the uncertainty of future events. TVM can be applied to transaction finance, but only if precise times or work-day requirements are known. Unfortunately, what we often do not know is the actual timing of each element in the transaction cycle. If we were to have this information, we could calculate IRR on the basis of the fraction of the year necessary for the completion of a cycle.

The reader is referred to any standard corporate or managerial finance text for a more complete discussion of this topic.

Chapter 4

TRANSACTION FINANCE CASE—GYZMO I

Experience, the universal Mother of Sciences.

—Miguel de Cervantes (1547–1616),
Don Quixote de la Mancha

Grahvell and Mope Manufacturing, Inc., NASDAQ symbol "GYZMO," designs, manufactures, and markets industrial and consumer products. The company has strong brand names, proprietary technology, and major market positions in two principal businesses: Tools and Components, and Process/ Environmental Controls.

Gyzmo was founded in 1964 by Mickey Mope and Gregory Grahvell, two young engineers who both graduated from Florida State University during the 1950s and became friends while working for an automotive parts manufacturer in Ohio. From

The Gyzmo case presented in the remainder of Part I and throughout Part II deals with a real company whose identity and locations have been changed, as have the names of all managers and other identifying factors.

A number of important topics are mentioned in Part I in the context of developing transaction finance concepts. In the interest of retaining the continuity of the case narrative, we defer the discussion of these topics until Part II. However, the interested reader should refer to the appropriate section if additional explanation is required.

their humble beginnings manufacturing carburetors for internal combustion engines in Springfield, Missouri, Mope and Grahvell were able to accelerate the company's growth with their timely strategic acquisitions and divestitures.

By 1999 Gyzmo's sales had climbed to $743.4 million, and net income reached $54.2 million. These figures represented the latest in a series showing continuous growth in sales and earnings since the company went public in 1988. Sales grew during the past five years at an average annual compound rate of 15.1%, while net income grew at an average annual compound rate of 152.1% during the same period.

In 1999 the return-on-sales was 7.2%, and the return-on-equity was 18.4%. Exhibit 4-1 presents selected financial highlights for the past five years, Exhibit 4-2 shows consolidated income statements for 1998–1999, and Exhibit 4-3 presents consolidated balance sheets for that period.

Product Lines

The Tools and Components (T&C) business segment manufactures and distributes a broad range of hand tools, tool holders, storage containers, hardware, wheel service equipment, fasteners, and components for consumer, industrial, and professional markets. Products are sold through retail channels; independent tool distributors; industrial, utility, and agricultural distributors; and original equipment manufacturers. T&C accounts for 60% of Gyzmo's total sales.

Typical hand tool customers range from do-it-yourselfers and professional/industrial end-users to auto mechanics. Component customers, generally original equipment manufacturers, include portable drill and heavy-duty diesel engine manufacturers. T&C comprises the following divisions and subsidiaries: Cool Tool Division and Ace Fastener and Squeaky Wheel Services Division, and products from this business segment are marketed under well-recognized brand names, including Terminator, Mangler, Facilitator, and Instigator. T&C gross margins have been level over the past three years because of the relative maturity of these product lines.

The Process/Environmental Controls (P/EC) business segment produces a broad range of monitoring, sensing, controlling, measuring, counting, and electrical power quality products, systems, and components. A major growth area and focus is environmental products. These products include inventory control and leak detection systems used to monitor underground fuel storage tanks and fuel pipelines.

P/EC products are distributed by the company's sales personnel and independent representatives to original equipment manufacturers, distributors, and other end-users. The segment's op-

Exhibit 4-1. Gyzmo selected financial highlights, 1995–1999.

($000s omitted, except per share data)	*1999*	*1998*	*1997*	*1996*	*1995*
Net revenues	743,385	556,987	468,817	422,842	367,212
Tools & components*	502,503	404,995	345,672	315,017	277,245
Process/environment controls*	240,882	151,992	123,145	107,825	89,967
Operating margins	90,129	62,214	43,529	29,450	18,475
Tools & components	53,997	40,935	27,520	16,511	8,579
Process/environment controls	36,132	21,279	16,009	12,939	9,896
Earnings (continuing operations)	52,883	36,160	24,015	15,222	8,360
Per share	1.77	1.24	0.83	0.53	0.29
Earnings from discontinued operations	1,275	4,666	2,860	579	(1,699)
Per share	0.04	0.16	0.10	0.02	−0.06
Net earnings	54,158	40,825	26,875	15,801	6,661
Per share	1.81	1.40	0.93	0.55	0.23
Dividends declared	2,336	1,855	1,706	0	0
Per share	0.08	0.065	0.06	0.00	0.00
Avg. common shares outstanding	29,922	29,161	28,897	28,728	28,959

*Large systems revenues are approximately as follows:
T&C—$175 million.
P/EC—$200 million.

Exhibit 4-2. Gyzmo consolidated statement of earnings, 1998–1999.

(000s omitted, except per share data)	*1999*	*1998*
Net revenues	$743,385	$556,987
Less: Cost of sales	$519,811	$395,937
Gross margin	$223,574	$161,050
Less: Selling, general, & administrative expense	$104,182	$77,559
EBITDA	$119,392	$83,491
Less: Depreciation expense	$29,264	$21,277
Operating profit (EBIT)	$90,129	$62,214
Less: Interest expense	$3,599	$1,601
Net income before taxes	$86,530	$60,613
Less: Income taxes	$33,647	$24,454
Net income	$54,158	$40,825
Average common shares outstanding	29,931	29,163
Net income per share	$1.81	$1.40

erating companies include Power 'n Go, Lean Green Machine, and Puddle Muddle. P/EC accounts for 40% of Gyzmo's sales. Gross margins have been steadily increasing for P/EC systems due to Gyzmo's superior reputation.

Marketing

Gyzmo sells both from inventory and on the basis of specific orders, depending on the product or system. Sales agents represent Gyzmo to global markets on a commission basis. They can quote prices, terms of delivery, and so on for standard products on the basis of company guidelines but must contact Gyzmo engineers to quote sophisticated P/EC and Squeaky Wheel systems. Customers include large hardware and discount chains, transportation companies, utilities, manufacturing companies, and a general variety of large and medium-size companies.

Exhibit 4-3. Gyzmo consolidated balance sheets, as of December 31.

(000s omitted)	1999	1998
ASSETS		
Cash and equivalents	$3,969	$1,800
Trade accounts receivable	$112,326	$84,080
Inventories (LIFO basis)	$100,945	$67,471
Prepaid expense and other	$15,995	$25,336
Total current assets	$233,235	$178,685
Property, plant, and equipment, net	$145,969	$122,084
Other assets	$59,722	$36,305
Excess of cost over net assets of acquired companies	$304,070	$215,750
Total assets	$742,996	$552,823
LIABILITIES & STOCKHOLDER'S EQUITY		
Notes payable and current portion of debt	$7,485	$34,386
Trade accounts payable	$46,145	$39,055
Accrued expenses	$148,439	$114,254
Total current liabilities	$202,069	$187,694
Long-term debt	$134,309	$58,258
Common stock ($0.01 per value)	$317	$316
Additional paid-in capital	$157,603	$155,824
Cumulative foreign translation adjustment	$1,799	$295
Retained earnings	$152,182	$100,360
Treasury stock (2,451,603 shares, at cost)	($18,745)	($18,745)
Total stockholder's equity	$293,156	$238,050
Total liabilities and stockholder's equity	$990,769	$679,904

The T&C business is price competitive, while the P/EC business is less so, given the required technology and expertise in the environmental controls business. Credit terms vary by business unit, with the P/EC business and the Squeaky Wheel division both requiring down payments for large systems, payment upon shipment, and final payment upon acceptance.

Business Unit	Down Payment	Payment at Shipment	Payment at Acceptance
P/EC	20%	70%	10%
Squeaky Wheel	30%	60%	10%

These conditions are somewhat loosely enforced. The other Gyzmo businesses bill net 30 or net on receipt, with days sales outstanding averaging 30–60 days.

Manufacturing and Distribution Facilities

T&C maintains manufacturing facilities in four sites:

> Cool Tool, Springfield, Missouri
> Ace Fastener, Fresno, California
> Squeaky Wheel, Jacksonville, Florida,
>   and Hartford, Connecticut

There are approximately 1,500 employees in the T&C segment, distributed about equally among the four sites. Each site maintains local banking arrangements for trade payables and payroll, and those accounts are also used for deposit of monies received from customers, who are instructed to remit payments to the manufacturing office.

P/EC business segment has three manufacturing facilities:

> Power 'n Go, Springfield, Missouri (power quality systems)
> Lean Green, Baltimore, Maryland (environmental products)
> Puddle Muddle, St. Paul, Minnesota (storage tank/pipeline monitoring)

The growth of environmental products is causing Gyzmo to consider opening a fourth production site, with both Texas and Tennessee under consideration. There are 1,000 employees in this segment, 500 in Springfield and 250 each in Baltimore and St. Paul. As with T&C, each site maintains local banking for trade payables, payroll, and collections. Fuel 'n Go instructs its customers to remit to a lockbox in San Francisco, recently established at that location because of the expected growth of the environmental business in California, but many customers still remit to Springfield.

Gyzmo's operating philosophy is to seek achievement of world-class excellence in customer satisfaction. Beginning with the "voice of the customer," the company strives to improve quality and timeliness of service, delivery, and cost. In support of this goal, the organizational structure is decentralized, with each operating unit responsible for all aspects of its business. An organization chart is shown in Exhibit 4-4.

The T&C business manufactures primarily for inventory on a continuous basis, but Squeaky Wheel Services is largely dependent on the activities of its sales force, which works with large transportation companies. The P/EC business is largely order-driven, although some standard products are held in inventory. (Squeaky Wheel and P/EC are referred to as "large systems" businesses throughout the case.)

Financial Structure

The debt-to-capital ratios for Gyzmo are 60.5% in 1999 and 56.9% in 1998. The average debt-to-capital ratio for Gyzmo's industry (specialized manufacturing) is 50%, with competitors' long-term debt issues selling at a 6% rate and equity issues at a 12% cost of capital.

Gyzmo's long-term debt consists of a new $150 million issue of 30-year corporate bonds with a coupon interest rate of 7.5% and a five-year-old $75 million issue of 10-year convertible bonds with a coupon interest rate of 3% (a 7.5% implicit cost) with conversion beginning in 1999 to common stock at $20/share. In addition, some older debt is being retired as required by the original loan agreement. Gyzmo can raise an additional $100 million in long-term debt capital at an estimated interest cost of 10%.

Exhibit 4-4. Organization chart.

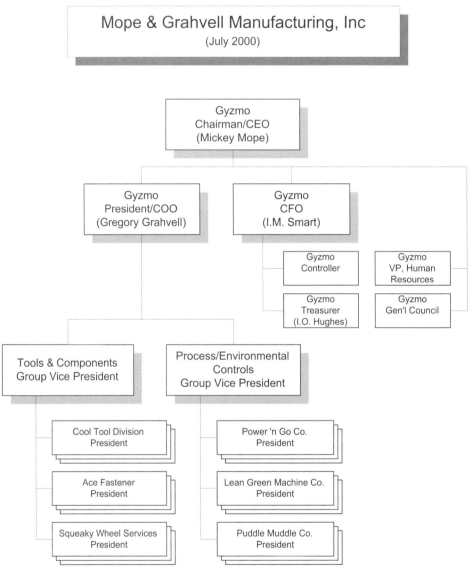

Gyzmo's stock price fluctuated in 1999 between $18 and $26 and traded most often at $22. In 1998, the stock traded between $20 and $30, with the price averaging $25. Gyzmo is currently paying 30¢/share in dividends, equivalent to about 1%, with the stock trading at $32. The estimated cost of a new stock issue is 16%, consisting almost entirely of the expected appreciation in the price of the shares.

Issues for the New CFO

Gyzmo recently hired its first Chief Financial Officer (CFO), I. M. Smart, an experienced financial executive who previously worked for Consolidated Colossal. Smart's mandate is to completely revamp the financial organization of the company, as appropriate. He is knowledgeable about recent developments in corporate finance, including cost of capital issues, capital budgeting, and theories of dividend policy. However, he is receiving conflicting advice from the commercial and investment banking communities, his accountants, and his barber.

Smart needs to clarify his current situation and develop an appropriate plan of action. He wonders if any mistakes have been made in the formulation of the company's capital structure. If so, what should the capital structure of the company be, and how can he help get the company there? The first step in determining the financial situation of Gyzmo is to determine the cost of capital, the calculation of which is shown in Exhibit 4-5.

Exhibit 4-5. Calculation of Gyzmo's cost of capital (debt capital costs are calculated on an after-tax basis).

	Gyzmo			Competitors		
	Capital Structure	*Capital Cost*	*Gyzmo's Cost*	*Capital Structure*	*Capital Cost*	*Competitors' Cost*
Current Structure						
Debt	0.610	0.050	.0305	0.500	0.040	0.0200
Equity	0.395	0.160	.0632	0.500	0.120	0.0600
Weighted capital cost			.0937			0.0800
Future Structure						
Debt	0.610	0.066	.0403			
Equity	0.395	0.160	.0632			
Weighted capital cost			.1035			

Note: The cost after tax of Gyzmo's current debt is 7.5% times (1–34%), or 50%.

The cost of capital is higher than optimal because of the high debt-to-capital ratio. The current capital structure is about $1^1/_3\%$ higher than the industry's weighted cost of capital ($9^1/_3\%$ vs. 8%) and would be $2^1/_3\%$ higher ($10^1/_3\%$ vs. 8%) should any additional debt be added. This additional annual cost is equivalent to about $5.85 million in the current structure, calculated as ($1^1/_3\%$) times ($427.5 million: the total of all financed capital). See Exhibit 4-3 for these data: $134.3 million in long-term debt and $293.2 million in stockholder's equity.

Gyzmo made the mistake of assuming that the explicit interest cost on its latest $75 million financing was cheaper than the implicit weighted cost of capital. That is, it accepted an apparently low cost of financing—debt at 5%[1]—versus equity at 16%; future debt costs are 6.6%. Competitors' after-tax debt costs are about 4%. However, the impact of a high proportion of debt is to drive the average cost of capital higher than it should be. The company must raise any additional capital required through equity: retained earnings and new common stock.

I. M. Smart's Review

The excellent financial results experienced by Gyzmo have not been reflected in the company's stock price. Mope and Grahvell hope that Smart's work with Consolidated Colossal will stimulate the changes necessary to release the intrinsic value of Gyzmo, including technological expertise and brand marketplace recognition. The two founders would also like to move toward an e-commerce platform, with marketing and purchasing conducted electronically.

Smart is concerned that Gyzmo is really attempting to manage very different businesses—traditional T&C products and Squeaky Wheel and P/EC large systems—and may not be fully appreciating the complexity of each operation. This is a particular concern given the geographic decentralization of the company. Stock market investors may be aware of these problems in their price evaluation of the company, and there has been some excitement at Smart's appointment given his previous successes.

1. The cost of debt capital is reduced by the assumed federal tax deduction, 34%.

Smart's requests for data specific to the various T&C and P/EC segments did not initially yield much insight into the various time-line activities and profitability. Gyzmo's financial data are aggregated into the traditional types of reports shown in Exhibits 4-1 through 4-3. There are budgeted costs for the various materials, labor, and overhead categories. However, discussions with production managers and accountants indicate that these costs do not reflect individual site or product situations and are based on budgeted estimates rather than actual results.

P/EC Transaction Finance Analysis

In order to properly analyze the situation, Smart began with a transaction finance analysis of the various P/EC divisions.[2] P/EC was generally agreed to be the most likely Gyzmo e-commerce business, given the extent of engineering and customization of environmental control systems. He requested details of the marketing and production of each P/EC activity but discovered that there was no current documentation of workflow or data concerning the timing of specific tasks. In order to develop the necessary information, Smart selected specific P/EC systems and had his team track the days and costs to complete each cycle.

The first step in developing this analysis was to list each of the work-day categories: sales, materials purchases, labor employed, manufacturing and administrative overhead, billing, and cash receipts. The dollars of known costs were listed for each of these time-line elements, as well as the actual work-days funds employed. An interest cost per day was calculated from Gyzmo's $9^{1}/_{3}\%$ cost of capital. On the basis of the capital allocated to the various P/EC business segments, Smart's team calculated critical transaction finance measures, the three ledger and time value of money (TVM) transaction finance returns: the gross margin percentage (GM percent), return-on-sales percentage (ROS percent), and return-on-equity percentage (ROE percent). The ledger calculations show traditional calculations without consideration of the TVM (or interest charge), while the TVM calculations include an imputed interest charge.

The results are provided in Exhibit 4-6 (with a detailed explana-

---

2. We defined "transaction finance" in Chapter 3 as the completion of financial arrangements for the sale of a business product or service.

Exhibit 4-6. Gyzmo P/EC summary of work-day requirements and transaction finance analysis.

	Monthly Amount ($000)	Payment to Vendor*	Total Inventory Days	Work-Days Funds Employed	Interest Cost/ Day	Total Interest Cost
Materials	$8,500	42	71	29	$2,182	$62,253
WIP: Labor & benefits	$7,000			35	$1,797	$62,253
WIP: Overhead	$1,600			35	$411	$14,222
Billing cycle	$17,100			12	$4,390	$51,214
Cash receipt to good funds**	$20,000			43	$5,134	$222,698
Allocated sales & marketing***	$1,000			9	$257	$2,315
Allocated genl. & administration***	$600			5	$154	$725
Total interest cost				167		$415,680
Allocated capital	$11,000					

WIP = Work in Progress.
*Including clearing of disbursement.
**Including accumulation of billing detail and preparation and mailing of invoice.
***Allocation of sales and marketing and general and administration expenses.
Source: See Exhibit 4-10.

tion in Exhibit 4-10) and demonstrate quite a mix of diverse activities involving numerous processing steps. While the assumed or "ledger" ROE is 11.8%, the TVM ROE is only 8.0% due to the length of the total cycle to complete all required business activities. Furthermore, Power 'n Go is the only segment providing a significant contribution to ledger and TVM ROE, with results of 16.3% and 11.0%, respectively. Each of the elements within the business cycle experienced extensive delays, contributing to this result. Lean Green Machine, the environmental products segment, required an astonishing 186 days to complete the timeline cycle, or about one-half of a year.

All three P/EC segments required some five months or more for completion, with delays in each portion of the timeline. Smart immediately realized that he could not hope to improve Gyzmo's financial performance without a detailed review of each P/EC activity and the careful management of related transaction finance activities. In reviewing the various elements, Smart and his team concluded that there were inefficiencies throughout.

Materials

The purchase of raw materials in anticipation of potential price increases, attractive price discounts, or anticipated commodity shortages may appear to be reasonable. However, funds employed in idle raw materials averaged 29 days for P/EC.[3] Partnering with major suppliers can assure Gyzmo of sources of materials supply without the necessity for more than an average two-week inventory. Careful examination of accounts payables practices indicate that vendors were being paid on the due date and, in certain situations, up to four days before the due date. Revising this practice to the more typical U.S. practice of payment 10 days or so after the due date provided additional savings.

Work-in-Process

Work-in-process (WIP) deficiencies were due to sub-optimal workstation design, which in turn led to problems in the physical movement of materials and delays at each manufacturing site. The average work-in-process was 35 days but varied from 25 days for Puddle Muddle to 40 days for Lean Green Machine. Workstation scheduling was particularly complicated for Lean Green because of intricate manufacturing and inspection processes prior to subsequent fabrication steps. Just-in-time practices would support more efficient work-in-process through the grouping of manufacturing cells, including equipment, to minimize travel distances. Quality control would minimize work stoppages and the holding of buffer or safety inventory should defective materials be discovered. Revisions to work-in-process flow could reduce average work-days by five days.

3. All calculations are dollar-weighted by accounting costs. Materials work-days are calculated on a net basis, that is, after deduction of the total holding period of the inventory less the period to the payment of the related vendor invoices.

Billing Cycle

Gyzmo has been reasonably effective in completing the billing cycle, which involves the assembly of data from various production work areas, the verification of the data, and the preparation of invoices. The average P/EC billing cycle time is 12 days. The outlier is Lean Green Machine at 15 days, largely because of the need to match draft invoices against contract requirements and limitations.

Smart discovered that the billing cycle was actually managed by the Information Systems Group, which determined that invoices would be printed at their convenience: every second Thursday at 3 A.M. This caused numerous delays in billing completed work and often resulted in up to a one-week lag in the receipt of the invoice by the customer. Revisions to the invoicing system could reduce data collection and review times by three days and generate customer bills more quickly.

Cash Receipts

The entire cash collection cycle involves customer invoice review, payment authorization, and the banking of funds received. P/EC needs an average of 43 work-days for the completion of cash receipts, with Puddle Muddle requiring 50 days. Smart's review indicated that Puddle Muddle provided multiple addresses on its bills, resulting in confusion among the customers' payable clerks and some misdirected items. Various actions may improve the cash receipts time, including "cleaner" invoices, lockboxing[4] at the optimal banks for Gyzmo's customer base, and the conversion of paper checks to electronic funds transfers.[5] Potential savings are about five days.

4. A lockbox is a collection mechanism in which mail containing payments bypasses corporate offices, going directly to a post office box maintained by the bank of deposit, thereby reducing collection float. For additional explanation, see Chapter 9.
5. Electronic funds transfers use technology to eliminate the paper instruments that are normally associated with the movement of money, including Fedwires (for same-day funds settlement) and ACHs (for next-day funds settlement). This is discussed in greater detail in Chapter 9.

Results of Smart's Review

There are opportunities to reduce work-days and improve returns throughout the timeline. Each segment must be investigated by the managers with the appropriate expertise, whether it be marketing, manufacturing, engineering, accounting, information systems, purchasing, or payroll. However, each segment contains a transaction finance component that must be included to define current and projected financial performance.

   The work-day benefits from the efforts of Smart and his team are summarized in Exhibit 4-7. The impacts from these changes are presented in Exhibits 4-8 and 4-9 (with details in Exhibit 4-10). The "ledger" results do not change because the various improvements relate to the timing of cost (and not revenue) events. However, the TVM ROS improves from 4.4% to 5.0%, and the TVM ROE increases

(text continues on page 95)

Exhibit 4-7. Gyzmo P/EC improvement opportunities.

Segment	Improvement Opportunities	Work-Day Reduction	Work-Day Savings
Materials	Reduction in idle inventory through partnering with suppliers	29 to 14	15
Materials	Payment of vendor invoices 10 days after the due date	28 to 40	12
Work-in-process	Just-in-time practices; quality control improvements	35 to 30	5
Billing cycle	Coordinate billing cycle with Information Systems Group	12 to 9	3
Cash receipts	Improve invoice design, use lockbox, collect by electronic funds transfers	43 to 36	7
	Total work-day improvements		**42**

Exhibit 4-8. P/EC work-days and returns after manufacturing changes.

	Monthly Amount	Work-Days Funds Employed	Cost/Day	Total Interest Cost
Materials	$8,500,000	2	$2,182	$4,364
WIP: Labor & benefits	$7,000,000	30	$1,797	$53,910
WIP: Overhead	$1,600,000	30	$411	$12,322
Billing cycle	$17,100,000	9	$4,390	$39,508
Cash receipt to good funds	$20,000,000	36	$5,134	$184,833
Allocated sales & marketing	$1,000,000	9	$257	$2,310
Allocated genl. & administration	$600,000	5	$154	$770
Total interest cost		121		$298,017
Allocated capital	$11,000,000			

Source: Developed from Excel spreadsheet detail similar to Exhibit 4-10.

Exhibit 4-9. Gyzmo P/EC before and after transaction finance results.

Measure	Before Actions	After Actions
Ledger GM%	14.5%	14.5%
TVM GM%	12.4%	13.0%
Ledger ROS%	6.5%	6.5%
TVM ROS%	4.4%	5.0%
Ledger ROE%	11.8%	11.8%
TVM ROE%	8.0%	9.1%
Total imputed interest cost	$415,680	$298,017

Exhibit 4-10. Gyzmo P/EC, detail of work-day requirements and transaction finance analysis.

	Monthly Amount	Terms	Payment to Vendor**	Total Inventory Days	Work-Days Funds Employed	Interest Cost/Day	Total Interest Cost
P/EC Summary*							
Materials	$8,500,000		42	71	29	$2,182	$62,253
WIP: Labor & benefits	$7,000,000				35	$1,797	$62,253
WIP: Overhead	$1,600,000				35	$411	$14,222
Billing Cycle	*$17,100,000*				12	$4,390	$51,214
Cash Receipt to Good Funds***	$20,000,000				43	$5,134	$222,698
Allocated Sales & Marketing^	$1,000,000				9	$257	$2,315
Allocated Genl. & Administration^	$600,000				5	$154	$725
Total Interest Cost					168		$415,680
Allocated Capital	$11,000,000						
Puddle Muddle							
Materials	$1,250,000	n/30	35	55	20	$321	$6,418
WIP: Labor & benefits	$1,500,000				25	$385	$9,627
WIP: Overhead	$300,000				25	$77	$1,925
Billing Cycle	*$3,050,000*				10	$783	$7,830
Cash Receipt to Good Funds***	$3,500,000	n/30			50	$898	$44,925
Allocated Sales & Marketing^	$200,000				9	$51	$438
Allocated Genl. & Administration^	$100,000				4	$26	$100
Total Interest Cost					143		$71,263
Allocated Capital	$2,500,000						
Lean Green Machine							
Materials	$2,400,000	n/30	40	70	30	$616	$18,483
WIP: Labor & benefits	$2,500,000				40	$642	$25,671
WIP: Overhead	$800,000				40	$205	$8,215
Billing Cycle	*$5,700,000*				15	$1,463	$21,949
Cash Receipt to Good Funds***	$6,500,000	n/30			45	$1,669	$75,088
Allocated Sales & Marketing^	$350,000				10	$90	$938
Allocated Genl. & Administration^	$200,000				5	$51	$271
Total Interest Cost					185		$150,615
Allocated Capital	$1,000,000						
Power 'n Go							
Materials	$4,850,000	n/30	45	75	30	$1,245	$37,352
WIP: Labor & benefits	$3,000,000				35	$770	$26,955
WIP: Overhead	$500,000				35	$128	$4,492
Billing Cycle	*$8,350,000*				10	$2,144	$21,435
Cash Receipt to Good Funds***	$10,000,000	n/30	40		40	$2,567	$102,685

Exhibit 4-10. (Continued)

	Monthly Amount	Terms	Payment to Vendor**	Total Inventory Days	Work-Days Funds Employed	Interest Cost/Day	Total Interest Cost
Allocated Sales & Marketing^	$450,000				8	$116	$934
Allocated Genl. & Administration^	$300,000				5	$77	$354
Total Interest Cost					163		$194,207
Allocated Capital	$4,000,000						

Billing cycle data are shown in italics as a sum of timeline segments. Cash receipt is the amount billed on these costs.
*All Summary work-days data are dollar-weighted
**Including clearing of disbursement
***Including accumulation of billing detail, preparation and mailing of invoice
^Allocation of sales and marketing, and general and administrative expenses, restated as days based on the total of manufacturing cycle days

P/EC Summary and Detail Work-Day and Transaction Results

The basis of transaction finance analysis is the determination of the costs to accomplish each of the elements in the manufacturing and non-manufacturing cycles by major business segment. These elements are defined as Materials; Work-in-Process (WIP) for direct labor and benefits and for overhead; Billing Cycle; Cash Receipts to Good Funds Receipt; Allocated Sales and Marketing; and Allocated General and Administration. These costs are discussed in detail in Part II.

The costs are evaluated by determining the number of work-days assigned to the completion of each element (cell D5). For the Materials element, it is necessary to deduct the number of days before payment is made to the vendor (cell E5) from the work-days that funds are actually employed (cell F5). This adjustment is not required for the other elements, as costs are assumed to be paid as incurred.

The number of work-days is determined by an evaluation of the time to complete each element. This is normally accomplished by sampling workflow activities for a representative period of time, using production records, invoices, receivables files, and general ledger accounting data. In order to completely describe all tasks and activities, it is frequently useful to document workflow activities.

The transaction finance calculations in the accompanying Excel spreadsheet are based on these cell formulae defined here for the P/EC Summary calculations. The cell formulae for the business segments within P/EC would be calculated in a similar manner.

Billing Cycle (B8) = Materials (B5) + WIP: Labor & benefits (B6) + WIP: Overhead (B7)
Work-Days Funds Employed (F5) = ((F16*B16)+(F27*B27)+(F38*B38))/(B16+B27+B38)
Interest Cost/Day (G5) = ((B5)/365)*0.0937 (Cost of capital)
Total Interest Cost (H5) = F5*G5

The calculation of the financial metrics are as follows:

Ledger GM % = (B9−B8)/B9
TVM GM % = (B9−B8−H12)/B9
Ledger ROS % = (B9−B8−B10−B11)/B9
TVM ROS % = (B9−B8−B10−B11−B12)/B9
Ledger ROE % = (B9−B8−B10−B11)/B13
TVM ROE % = (B9−B8−B10−B11−H12)/B13
Total Interest Cost (H12) = SUM(H5:H11)

Standard spreadsheet notation is as follows:

Letters	=	columns
Number	=	rows
*	=	multiplication
/	=	division
−	=	subtraction
+	=	addition
:	=	the range of designated cells

to 9.1% from 8.0%. While these results do not yet achieve the target returns normally expected for businesses, usually an ROE in excess of 10 to 12%, they do represent the beginning of a substantial improvement over current performance and nearly cover the company's cost of capital.

Smart and other senior managers will next have to decide if the P/EC business can eventually earn a satisfactory return in the context of competition, customer demand, and other critical issues. Cooperation between the various disciplines is required, as well as leadership by senior management (Mope and Grahvell) and a continuous effort to accomplish desired margins. The only alternative to a failure to mount a coordinated effort may be to increase prices (which are usually set by market forces) or to abandon business segments and product lines.

The transaction finance approach used at Gyzmo can be used both in projecting business segment and product returns and in ascertaining the reasons for failures to achieve profitability targets. This discussion emphasizes the planning role, as management did not adequately consider timeline implications prior to the expenditure of capital. It is important to confer with the disciplines responsible for each timeline portion to ascertain reasonable work-day requirements, a reality check too often disregarded in the frantic work of business management.

TRANSACTION FINANCE CASE—GYZMO II

Wavering between the profit and the loss
In this brief transit where the dreams cross
The dream crossed twilight between birth and dying . . .

—T. S. Eliot (1888–1965), *Ash-Wednesday*

After conferring with Gyzmo's senior managers, Mr. Smart became convinced that the company's future lay with the P/EC business, with the T&C segment more of a mature "cash cow." The other managers were astonished to realize how marginal the P/EC business was in terms of current returns but were quick to agree that the various changes would be beneficial. They pledged their support and cooperation in implementing Smart's recommendations.

However, this did not solve the larger problem facing Smart and Gyzmo: how to make P/EC as profitable as T&C. Furthermore, P/EC was almost entirely composed of systems and not of standard products, making pricing, terms of delivery, and customization particularly difficult to manage (and a principal contributor to the mediocre margins). Smart was also concerned that P/EC's U.S. technological competitive advantage could be weakened as global trade and Internet information transfer expanded.

Sales, Order Entry, and Receivables Activities

The Smart team met to review these concerns and decided that more specific information was required to understand the P/EC transaction cycle. Exhibit 5-1 lists the data developed by the team, including the typical sales, order entry, and receivables cycle for power quality and environmental control systems. After reviewing these activities, Smart's team realized that there were very significant time delays in these various work cycles.

Exhibit 5-1. P/EC sales/order entry/receivables activities.

1. Sales representatives call on potential and current customers to discuss Gyzmo's products and systems. These efforts are supported by sales booths at conferences and shows, advertising in technical magazines, direct mail, and other promotions.
2. Requests-for-quote or purchase orders are obtained from potential buyers at the time that a decision is made to install power quality or environmental control systems.
3. Quotes are developed by marketing groups within business segments on the basis of standard costing and expected competitive pricing and mailed to customers or sales representatives.
4. Marketing groups determine the credit terms to be provided on the customer order. Standard terms are net 30 days. If credit is not provided to the customer, cash in advance of shipment is required.
5. Orders over $5,000 are reviewed by Corporate Credit for credit approval (once credit approval has been established); orders under $5,000 are not individually reviewed. Should Corporate Credit reject a credit or require guarantees by letters of credit, the senior management of each business can override that recommendation and approve a sale.
6. Orders are key-entered by clerks in each business unit directly to the order entry system (OES). Each order entry contains the order number, customer number, pricing and terms, and information specific to that order, in addition to product descriptions and codes.
7. OES provides manufacturing instructions to the factory for each customer order by computer printout. In addition, OES maintains product warranty information.
8. Upon shipment of the goods, OES generates multiple invoice copies, which are printed overnight after shipment and mailed by first-class regular mail. Copies are sent to Contracts, Manufacturing, and Customer Support. In those circumstances where credit was not granted to the customer, cash in advance of shipment or a letter of credit drawdown is required.
9. Terms and typical "progress" payment requirements vary by business unit. Customer payments are directed to lockboxes at Last National Bank or office addresses, both of which are printed on customer invoices.
10. On a daily basis, Last National Bank prepares a package of materials from each day's deposit that includes photocopies of all checks deposited, copies of deposit tickets, and invoices and other correspondence received at the lockbox.
11. Lockbox remittance media are sent by overnight courier to each business unit and are received by mid-morning. (Remittance media accompanying checks received at Gyzmo offices are retained with check copies for processing.)
12. Check copies and remittance media (when available) are used to apply cash versus open receivables on OES. Remittance documents used to apply payments include live checks, photocopies of checks, invoices, and wire transfer notifications.

The Sales Process

Business had historically been conducted on a "friendship" basis, involving lengthy discussions of the P/EC systems and the customer's requirements. These conversations might be conducted at the customer's site, or at an entertainment event such as a meal, baseball game, or golf outing. (Smart wondered about those $150 customer lunches he had to approve for reimbursement.) In addition, the sales force constantly lobbied for more promotional activities, particularly trade shows and conferences. (Come to think of it, those events always involved the wining and dining of sales prospects.)

The sales process was so lengthy that months might pass before a request-for-quote or purchase order was received. Whether a request-for-quote or purchase order, P/EC managers had to review each element of the buyer's requirements to determine whether the required conditions and pricing could be met given the production status of other orders, the cost and availability of materials, and scheduling constraints. Buyers frequently demanded discounts from list (standard) prices, reduced down payments, extended payment terms, or other concessions that had the effect of reducing revenue.

Credit Review

Credit review was similarly convoluted. As noted in Exhibit 5-1, each P/EC marketing group determined the customer's credit terms, with standard terms net 30 days. Certain customers were deemed desirable even though of questionable credit-worthiness, and in those situations rules could be relaxed. For other customers, rules were enforced, and sales required a letter of credit facility[1] or cash payment prior to shipment. Credit review varied by the amount of the order, with smaller orders (usually for replacement parts) accepted without the need for credit approval. In any event, the process was time-consuming, and no one was certain who would be approved (or even what the rules were).

1. A letter of credit is issued by a commercial bank to pay the seller of goods and services once certain conditions of sale are met. It is used to guarantee payment by poor domestic credit risks and in many international transactions.

Order Entry

The order entry process was established when the P/EC business was established and was based on a system used by T&C. Each accepted order was keyed into the order entry system (OES). OES required full enumeration of all product, customer, and order data, although many of these records could have been copied from other files. OES then issued printed instructions to the manufacturing facilities, including parts manifests, standard labor, production times and setups, and other data.[2]

Receivables Processing

Once the P/EC systems were ready for shipment to the customer, OES prepared multiple invoicing copies for each business group involved in completing the transaction. When the customer paid, by check either to the lockbox or to the appropriate Gyzmo company office, a copy of the invoice was typically sent with the check. These media were then used to apply cash received against the open accounts receivable in OES. If an invoice copy was not included with the payment, billing clerks had to determine where the payment belonged and whether it was in full or partial settlement of the account. In some cases payments were net of items in dispute.

Non-Manufacturing Work-Day Issues

Every one of these sales, order entry, and receivables activities was essential, yet each one involved time, repetitive actions, and considerable manager or clerical input. "Accommodations" could be made for special situations, but were these in the best interest of Gyzmo? (In one case, the U.S. government requested that consideration be given to the sale of a power quality system to an independent republic of the former Soviet Union, although no guarantees were provided. The company is still awaiting payment.)

Furthermore, a pricing discount could be offered by one manager, special quality standards accepted by another manager, and an extra 30 days for payment permitted by a third manager. Yet no one oversaw the transaction to ensure that intended margins were

2. Manufacturing considerations were discussed in Chapter 4.

being met. And, judging from Smart's analysis, the majority of P/EC transactions did not achieve these targets. The 14 days of average non-manufacturing time[3] (nine days of allocated sales and marketing and five days of general and administrative time) was necessary to accomplish all of the tasks enumerated in Exhibit 5-1 but costly both in the price of these activities and in the implicit interest expense.

The Sales Cycle

The elapsed time devoted to sales activities was often measured in months (and occasionally years), although only nine work-days were allocated according to accounting data. This time could be reduced only if buyers decided to more quickly proceed with P/EC system expenditures. A critical element in motivating faster purchase decisions was to understand buyer objections, which Smart resolved to do through joint customer visits with Gyzmo sales agents. However, once a purchase order or request-for-quote occurred, the process of developing quotes could be established on the basis of pricing rules set into a quoting system.

Smart's team was pondering these possibilities when a sales agent notified senior management about new competitive developments. One of his U.S. prospects had been considering a power quality system and had reviewed the Internet for companies that provided the technology it required. Six companies had Websites listing their capabilities, geographic markets served, years of experience, and technical specifications. Four of the competitors were located in Europe or the Far East and would not be able to readily serve the customer's needs. The other two were in North America (one U.S. and one Canadian) and could meet the buyer's various requirements. And the sales agent had been working with this prospect for five months!

Gyzmo Goes E-Commerce

Smart realized that e-commerce could erode his competitive position in P/EC systems by allowing additional, qualified companies

---

3. "Non-manufacturing time" refers to sales and marketing, and general and administrative time, and is stated on the income statement as expenses reducing gross margin to calculate profits before taxes.

to market to his customers and prospects at substantially lower cost than those Gyzmo incurred by having his sales team conduct ''explanatory'' visits (including entertainment). He discussed the situation with the senior management team that was dimly aware of e-commerce possibilities—one had recently read an article on e-commerce in *Business Week*. Although skeptical, they agreed to have the leading e-commerce technology companies submit proposals for the construction of a Gyzmo Website. The project was finally awarded to 2BorNOT2B.com.

Website Features

The site (www.gyzmo.com) took five months to construct, secure, and test using past P/EC transactions. (E-commerce security issues are discussed in the chapter appendix.) Gyzmo executives and 2Bor-NOT2B.com discovered that the previous work by Smart's group[4] enabled the e-commerce team to construct alternative power quality systems models, including the various manufacturing elements, pricing, scheduling and delivery requirements, and other customer service issues. Furthermore, an e-commerce site minimized the time required to complete most of the steps in the sales, order entry, and receivables cycle.

  For example, as Smart suspected, requests-for-quotes and the input of customers' purchase orders could be input directly from the new e-commerce Website to a quoting/order entry/production scheduling system, saving an average of three days. Similarly, credit arrangements could be established from formal rules as supplemented from Dun and Bradstreet credit reporting information. This saved an estimated one day of credit review, as well as standardizing the credit approval process.

Website Transactions

Invoices could be generated from OES data and sent electronically to customers and interested P/EC groups, saving one additional day of processing time (and two to three days of mail time). Cash could be applied to open accounts receivable from bank downloads without the necessity to refer to paper remittance documents, sav-

4. As discussed in Chapter 4.

ing two days. The total savings in the sales, order entry, and receivables activities became seven days, a 50% reduction in non-manufacturing time.

The e-commerce site provided the further advantage of minimizing transaction mistakes. Although improvements were implemented in the initial phases of Smart's review, there continued to be the possibility that these changes could be ignored due to individual error, complacency, favoritism for a particular customer or sales agent, or in special circumstances. Standard rules made those deviations possible but difficult, since the decision models had to be deliberately circumvented. Finally, the selling process was expedited as customers and prospects could find Gyzmo through the Internet and initiate serious inquiries.

The dramatic effects on P/EC returns are shown in Exhibit 5-2 (with details in Exhibit 5-3). The benefits to Gyzmo from Smart's initial efforts were entirely from imputed interest savings (reflected in TVM returns). Each manufacturing task remained, although considerably less time was required (150 manufacturing work-days were reduced to 107 work-days). The second phase of Smart's review (as discussed throughout this chapter) directly impacted both sales and marketing and general and administrative days, resulting in significant benefits. Total P/EC (manufacturing and non-manufacturing) work-days declined from 167 to 114 days, an improvement of more than 30%.

Change Impacts on Gyzmo Stock

As we noted in the first part of this case, Mr. Smart was hired to improve Gyzmo's stock price—to maximize shareholder value. By

Exhibit 5-2. Changes in TVM (time value of money) returns.

	Prior to Changes	*After Initial Changes*	*After E-Commerce Changes*
TVM GM%	12.4%	13.0%	13.0%
TVM ROS%	4.4%	5.0%	9.0%
TVM ROE%	8.0%	9.1%	16.4%

Exhibit 5-3. P/EC work-days and returns after non-manufacturing changes.

	Monthly amount	Work-Days Funds Employed	Cost/Day	Total Interest Cost
Materials	$8,500,000	2	$2,182	$4,364
WIP: Labor & benefits	$7,000,000	30	$1,797	$53,910
WIP: Overhead	$1,600,000	30	$411	$12,322
Billing cycle	$17,100,000	9	$4,390	$39,508
Cash receipt to good funds	$20,000,000	36	$5,134	$184,833
Allocated sales & marketing	$555,550	5	$143	$713
Allocated genl. & administration	$240,000	2	$62	$123
Total interest cost		114		$295,773
Allocated capital	$11,000,000			

Source: Developed from Excel spreadsheet detail similar to Exhibit 4-10.

instituting various changes to P/EC, the earnings per share for 1999 (from continuing operations) increased from $1.77 to $2.21 (on a pro forma basis). Impacts to selected components of the company's consolidated statement of earnings are provided in Exhibit 5-4.

The improvement in per share earnings and margins, together with the transformation of P/EC to an e-commerce business, impressed the stock market community. The price-earnings of Gyzmo stock (now Gyzmo.com) increased from 18 times ($32 ÷ $1.77) to 24 times, resulting in a common stock price of $53 (24 times $2.21). The markets anticipated significant additional power quality and environmental control system business, particularly because of the success of Gyzmo's e-commerce Website.

Mr. Smart convinced Grahvell and Mope to use the additional $12 million of earnings to reduce long-term debt in order to begin to reduce the company's cost of capital. Smart hoped to move Gyzmo

Exhibit 5-4. Significant consolidated statement of earnings results (pro forma, before and after changes to P/EC business segment).

| | Prior to Changes | | | After Changes | |
	Gyzmo	T&C	P/EC	P/EC	Gyzmo
Dollars					
Net revenues	$743,385	$446,031	$297,354	$297,354	$743,385
Less: cost of sales	$519,811	$289,920	$229,891	$229,891	$519,811
Gross margin	$223,574	$156,111	$67,463	$67,463	$223,574
Net income	$54,158	$34,830	$19,328	$31,222	$66,052
Net income per share	$1.77	$1.06	$0.71	$1.15	$2.21
Percentages					
Gross margin*	30.1%	35.0%	22.7%	22.7%	30.1%
Net income	7.3%	7.8%	6.5%	10.5%	8.9%

*Large systems target gross margins: T&C = 15%; P/EC = 20%.

toward the 50% debt/50% equity balance sheet that would minimize the company's cost of capital. This move was supported by his commercial and investment bankers. While the early retirement of debt saved only about $600,000 in after-tax interest costs, this step led investors to respect management's sense of fiscal responsibility and to raise the common stock's price-earnings to 26 times earnings, equal to a market price of $57 a share.

Gyzmo Sells Stock

An invigorated Gyzmo not only pleased the investment community but thrilled Mope and Grahvell, whose personal holdings had risen more than 75% in value. With his new wealth, Mope decided to endow a chair in e-commerce engineering at his alma mater, Florida State. Grahvell wanted to use his money to buy a home in the Florida Keys. However, neither wanted to sell stock in the open market, which might disturb the supply-demand relationship and cause the price to fall.

Both men mentioned these wishes to I. M. Smart during a celebration dinner at the best restaurant in Springfield. Smart decided that his latest idea would segue nicely with the personal plans of his bosses: to sell a secondary issue of Gyzmo common stock from Treasury stock (see Exhibit 4-3) and from the holdings of Mope and Grahvell.

At the current price of $57, less the standard fees to underwriters, accountants, and attorneys (about 8%), a secondary would net about $52, or about $150 million if all Treasury stock and some of Mope and Grahvell's personal holdings were sold. The company could actively use about $125 million for investment projects, and, at the advice of the underwriters, this was the amount chosen for sale.

Capital Structure Impact

As shown in Exhibit 5-5, the impact on the capital structure of Gyzmo of such a stock sale would be dramatic, bringing the company in line with its competitors and reducing the weighted cost of capital by about $1^1/_3$%. Extrapolating from competitors' cost of capital,[5] Gyzmo's costs would be reduced annually by about $7 million on a $540.5 million base of all financed capital ($427.5 million, less $12.0 million of redeemed debt and $125.0 million of the equity secondary).

Exhibit 5-5. Projected effects of $125 million stock issuance.

	1999 Capital Structure		Pro Forma 2000 Capital Structure*	
Debt	$449.8	60.5%	$437.8	51.0%
Equity	$293.2	39.5%	$420.6	49.0%
Total	$743.0	100.0%	$858.4	100.0%

*Assumes no other changes in the capital structure other than the redemption of $12 million of long-term debt.

5. See Exhibit 4-5, p. 85.

The secondary equity offering was co-managed by two of the leading investment banks and was successfully completed late in September 2000. The company realized $100 million from the sale, money that would eventually be used for the desired fourth production site for the environmental products business of P/EC; to acquire several manufacturing and distribution facilities from Sunbeam Corporation for the T&C business (at a substantial discount from the cost to construct equivalent facilities); and to begin serious expansion planning for global expansion based on new e-commerce opportunities.

The founders split the other $25 million: Mope endowed the engineering chair at FSU, and Grahvell bought a vacation home in Key Largo. For his efforts, Smart was named the new president of Gyzmo and received a substantial increase in his compensation package.

Lessons Learned

Mr. Smart was invited to speak at a meeting of the Association of Financial Professionals, a financial executives conference, in the fall of 2000, and as he was looking for an excuse to leave Springfield for a few days, he accepted. While Gyzmo had become a success by a re-orientation to the requirements of the new economy, Smart wondered what message he could distill from his recent experiences. The initial phase of his work clearly indicated that the company did not focus on time value of money issues in managing revenues and costs and that finance did not get sufficiently involved in sales and manufacturing activities.

He believed that financial executives had to "partner" with line functions to fully appreciate the interaction of the timeline concerns of other disciplines. Financial staff should be encouraged to leave the friendly confines of their department and actually find out what those numbers on the computer screen mean. Their job responsibilities should require visits on sales prospects to learn what customers and salespeople are saying and whether they are even listening to each other! Financial staff should be required to visit the production floor to observe a manufacturing process and to learn about typical problems and delays.

New Concerns of Finance

Smart noted that there were several areas of the business organization that require attention, even though once considered beyond finance's responsibility.

• *Sales.* Traditional marketing processes involves sales visits, customer entertainment, trust developed through years of relationship building, promotional events, and other costly, time-consuming activities. New economy opportunities will focus on broader markets and competition and on faster decision times, requiring a greater focus on the investment in sales efforts.

• *Invoice Generation.* Often a shared responsibility of sales, receivables (credit), and systems, the billing cycle may be managed on the basis of access to the invoicing system, without regard to the optimal timing of the printing/mailing process. Many companies invoice weeks later than optimal, with the result that their days sales outstanding is longer than the average for their industry.

• *Purchasing and Payables.* Finance managers should examine the adequacy of documentation and the invoice review process, any missed opportunities for volume purchasing, controls over access to approved vendor files, and whether payments are issued on appropriate dates.

• *Risk and Control.* Risk is integral to the responsibilities of the treasurer, *the* position in a business designated to safeguard its cash and other assets. However, every manager with responsibility for timeline elements must be cognizant of the various risks related to those activities and must be prepared to take action to manage the risks along with other organizational tasks. The dissemination of data throughout computing facilities and files makes regular backup and protection difficult to control, and the proliferation of internal and external data sources adds significant complexity to this process.

Smart realized that the financial executives probably wanted to hear about Gyzmo's success with e-commerce. However, the changes in P/EC showed that technology was potentially a dangerous tool if used without careful preparation and an in-depth understanding of costs and customer service issues. After reading over his remarks, Smart wondered if he sounded too preachy.

Chapter 5 Appendix

INTERNET SECURITY

The dependence of Internet sellers and buyers for accurate information on products and services creates a significant possibility of the compromise of that information. It is therefore necessary that each e-commerce Website take responsibility for its own protection and safety.

Basic Security Design

Because of the risk of intrusion, Websites should be insulated and protected to minimize the potential consequences of such attacks. Sites that are externally visible should be severed from the company's internal systems and connected only through secure, hard-wired local communications lines. A security perimeter should be established to contain all internal systems, and access should be through monitored entry points secured by multiple devices. Any sign of a breach of security should trigger the switch to a back-up site and a report of the attack to appropriate authorities. Although malevolent attacks are investigated and prosecuted, there is no central controlling authority or designated function to monitor potential intrusions.

Types of Attacks

Intrusions may be of any the following types:

• *Theft of Services.* Intruders "purchase" goods or services using disguises to hide their actual identities. This is a particular concern in e-commerce, as payment in most industries follows the delivery of product by some period of time. While credit checks and other investigation may disclose such intentions, a clever thief will have appropriated sufficient legitimate identification to fool the unsuspecting seller.

• *Flooding.* Concerted action by groups of intruders may attempt to flood sites with messages, which can overwhelm and temporarily close down service. The motive may be revenge, mischief, or the desire to do economic harm while aiding a competitor. (Harmless undesired messages are known as "spam.")

• *Domain Registrations.* Legitimate trademarks and organizational names may be used for purposes other than those in common usage and understanding, leading to ambiguity and the potential for mischief or blackmail to end the practice.

• *Unauthorized Disclosure.* Confidential data used in e-commerce transactions (e.g., competitive data, credit card numbers, passwords, personal information known only to the user) may be stolen and used for fraudulent activities.

• *Disturbance to the Network.* E-commerce business assumes that the Internet is available for communication between buyers and sellers. However, the network infrastructure may be disrupted or unavailable for a variety of innocent and sinister reasons, delaying potentially time-critical actions.

• *Inadequate Encryption.* Hackers attempt to eavesdrop on sensitive communications. There have been instances where such attacks have succeeded where encryption and authentication procedures have been inadequate, although known problems have been corrected.

Firewalls and Encryption

The vulnerability that results from these intrusions may not be obvious to the computer user, but it has resulted in countless incidents of eavesdropping, hacking, and theft. There are various types of barriers that should be constructed to protect e-commerce integrity. Firewall barriers force all communications to pass through the firewall, to protect internal communications from outsiders (or portions of internal systems from other internal networks). The firewall reviews all traffic and refuses entry to those who do not meet predetermined criteria.

Encryption involves the coding of data into indecipherable streams of gibberish (''ciphertext'') using an algorithm or mathematical formula that is translated according to a key known to the sender and receiver. Authentication involves determining that the sender and receiver are who they say they are (i.e., not a hacker listening in to a transmission of data) and that the message is as originally sent (i.e., not modified). Any sensitive data can be encrypted, but the process is most often used with data being transmitted through the Internet.

Various standard keys are used in encryption, and a major concern in selecting and managing the process is to control the distribution and management of these keys to protect against intrusion. Messages are encrypted through public and private asymmetric keys. The public key is publicly distributed, while the private key is kept secret. Data encrypted with the public key requires decryption with the private key, and data with a private key encryption can be read only by using the public key.

Despite these safeguards, e-commerce security is not certain. A recent survey reported that half of companies using e-commerce do not have a formal security policy.[6] In fact, three computer system providers in mid-1999 reported that certain Internet fire-wall protections were compromised and were invisible to standard antivirus programs.[7] The most susceptible users were certain Microsoft Office Suite users and Compaq and Hewlett-Packard owners whose computers upgrade automatically over the Internet to the manufacturer's software.

Other Barriers

In addition to installing firewalls and encryption/authentication software, it is necessary to protect telecommunications cabling. Telecommunications cables can be wiretapped at nearly any point, inside or outside your premises, allowing the display and recording

6. Carol Power, ''Business Seen Overconfident of E-Commerce Security,'' *American Banker*, February 8, 2000, p. 11.
7. John Markoff and Sara Robinson, ''Security Flaws in Software Are Reported,'' *New York Times*, July 31, 1999, pp. C1, C14.

of any information being exchanged. Taps can be placed at panels, in walls, at junction boxes, and in tubing placed in dropped ceilings and raised floors prepared for electronic equipment installations. Such cables should be encased in steel or pressure-sensitive conduits; the latter safeguard signals when there has been an intrusion on the line.

In addition to the use of commercially available packages for Internet sites, computer security requires continuous monitoring of alerts and information provided by companies and the media (including Websites, user groups, and other sources of computer news). Concern for the deliberate intrusion of computer systems has led to proposals for government monitoring of non-military and private-sector installations.

Part II

Process Metrics and Transaction Cycles

I wonder what goes on in this company?

Process metrics are used to evaluate the major transaction cycle elements. Chapters 6 through 9 address manufacturing cycles, Chapter 10 reviews marketing and administrative cycles, and Chapter 11 discusses service industry cycles.

Chapter 6

MATERIALS PURCHASES

Dirty British coaster with a salt-caked smokestack,
Butting through the Channel in the mad March days,
With a cargo of Tyne coal,
Road rail, pig lead,
Firewood, ironware, and cheap tin trays.

—John Masefield (1878–1967), *Cargoes*

Materials purchases involves the decision to purchase, and then paying for the purchase through the accounts payable function. Paper-driven old economy processes are among the first of the transaction cycles to be replaced by e-commerce systems, leading the migration to the new economy.

Old Economy Purchasing

Old economy purchasing is wasteful and time-consuming for both vendors and buyers. Suppliers suffer from labor-intensive order fulfillment processes, which are often error-prone and inefficient. Significant resources may be dedicated to the manual entry of information from faxed or phoned-in purchase orders (P.O.'s) and the manual processing of shipping notices and invoices. The cost of sales and customer acquisition may be excessive, including the production and distribution of paper catalogs, supplements, updates, and price lists.

The buyer typically requires a complex, multistep process for purchasing. See Exhibit 6-1 for elements of the purchasing cycle and opportunities for e-commerce applications. The various activities include requisitions and approvals by the requesting unit; reviews, solicitation of bids, and issuance of the P.O. by the purchasing department; shipment and invoicing by the vendor; matching of the P.O., receiving report, and the invoice by accounts payable; and issuance of the payment as approved by accounts payable and managed by a treasury unit. If the payment is by check, the cashed check must be reconciled against an issued file at month-end. Disputes arising

Exhibit 6-1. Purchasing cycle activities (from the perspective of the buying company).

Department	Activity	E-C*
Buying Company (prior to acquisition)		
Initiating business unit	Perception of product/service requirement	N
	Preparation of requisition	Y
	Manager approval as to need and budget capacity	Y
	Transmittal to Purchasing Dept.	Y
Purchasing Dept.	Requisition review/approval	Y
	Specification developed of product/service	Y
	Selection of vendor	N
	Preparation of purchase order with copy to Payables Dept.	Y
	Transmittal to vendor	Y
Selling Company		
	Acknowledgment of purchase order	Y
	Acquire, make, or pull from inventory	N
	Shipping to buying company, including documentation	N
	Issuance of invoice and establish receivables	Y
	Deposit or notification of payment receipt	**
	Application of cash to open receivables	Y
Buying company (after acquisition)		
Receiving Dept.	Receipt of shipment and documentation	N
	Preparation of receiving report and transmittal to Payables Dept.	Y
	Delivery of product to initiating business unit	N
	Receipt and matching of receiving report, purchase order, invoice, shipping documentation	Y
Payables Dept.	Authorization of payment	Y
Treasury Dept.	Issuance of payment (and funding and reconciliation of bank accounts)	**

*Subject to e-commerce application?
**These activities can be managed through electronic treasury mechanisms.

from incorrect quantities shipped, the condition of the materials received, or other problems can result in a lengthy resolution process. Such disagreements can involve numerous other documents, and significant time and effort.

Estimates of the cost per paper-based procurement range from $75 to $150, often exceeding the cost of the items being purchased. Transactions occur in a complex, paper-intensive request, approval, and order sequence, with high administrative costs and few economies of scale. These procedures often include the re-keying of information and the involvement of manufacturing and engineering personnel, often resulting in delays to end users and productivity losses.

The complete P.O. process is not always followed, and our experience is that about one-third of all purchases do not have a complete file of documents. Purchasing according to established procedures usually includes essential, repetitive purchases, such as paper, shipping materials, and office supplies, and equipment and furniture. The process is incomplete most often for specialized or technical products, such as computers and software, and for scientific or engineering instruments.

While it may be expedient to allow established procurement methods to become more permissive, purchase orders are valuable controls against vendor and employee problems. Supplier difficulties may develop, including pricing changes, slippage in delivery times, or quality issues, and fraudulent internal actions are easier in the absence of a formal P.O.

Local Purchasing and "Maverick Buying"

Many companies allow decentralized purchasing at multiple locations to maintain goodwill with the local business community, to "empower" on-site managers, or simply from indifference. Individual business units order directly from vendors in "emergencies" because they wish to reward certain vendors, or because of an unresponsive, somewhat bureaucratic central purchasing department. This practice, often referred to as "maverick buying," occurs when personnel do not follow internal guidelines as to which suppliers to use for operating purchases. Companies unable to leverage procurement economies of scale expend unnecessary amounts both on the purchasing function and on the items acquired.

It has been estimated that maverick buying accounts for one-third of operating resource expenditures, costing organizations a 15% to 25% premium on those purchases. In addition, low visibility into spending patterns further limits the benefits of volume procurement contracts. These purchases typically include arrangements for meetings and conferences, small package couriers, film developing, hardware and paint for maintenance, displays and exhibits, systems support including repairs and software, temporary services, and books and magazines. As a result of these decisions, multiple payments are often made for similar products and services.

Improved management of local purchasing may result in the following benefits:

- Quantity discounts for consolidated procurement from a few designated vendors
- Standardized purchases meeting specifications as to form, content, quality, time of delivery, and price
- Improved forecasting of purchasing requirements and determination of economic order quantity

Purchasing Cards

The requirement to access local sources of supply has stimulated the use of purchasing (or procurement) cards. These "credit" cards are issued through a bank or vendor to companies whose managers make small local purchases. The issuer can provide daily electronic information on the previous day's activities, by individual user, location, amount, merchant, and transaction type. Various limitations can be imbedded in codes in the card technology, such as daily dollar amount or restrictions on the types of purchases. Any unapproved activity is rejected when the card is presented to a merchant for payment.

Purchasing cards significantly reduce the cost of local purchasing while increasing the level of controls imposed by management. The primary savings are in reduced paperwork, but this is offset somewhat by lost opportunities for volume discounts. Employees are empowered and may receive a "psychic" benefit with this increased responsibility. The most significant barrier to the cards' use continues to be the entrenched opposition of purchasing departments, which perceive a diminution in their organizational role. Another disadvantage is the 1 to 2% charge to vendors that is assessed for the services of card issuers. These fees are for the settlement of funds transfer and the risk assumption in advancing funds to the seller while awaiting payment from the buyer.

Positive corporate experience with purchasing cards has resulted in a very significant decline in traditional buying. For example, one organization reports that 40,000 purchases declined to about 5,000 after use of the card was implemented.[1] Paper-based purchasing required four hours of processing and eight days of elapsed time for small-dollar items, including preparing the requisition and the P.O., receiving vendor bids, processing the receiver and the invoice, obtaining internal approvals, and routing paperwork. The card program reduced ordering time to a few minutes by telephone or a few hours at an approved vendor. Similar results have been re-counted by other companies.

Some companies examine each vendor relationship to determine whether the use of purchasing cards or the traditional P.O. process is more cost-effective. For example, it may be more efficient to interact by purchasing card with vendors who have a large numbers of invoice line items and to use P.O.'s with vendors from which a few, large line items are bought. Similarly, there is an unresolved tension between the percentage fee charged on purchasing card transactions and the small flat fee charged by funds transfer systems such as the ACH or paper check. This tension is likely to be eventually reconciled by lowered purchasing card fees.

Improvement in Old Economy Purchasing

Companies with a traditional P.O. process can institute various efficiencies, including the following:

- The dollar threshold for automatic approvals can be increased with only slight risk to the integrity of the purchasing process.
- Approvals can be against budgets without manager intervention. This eliminates the need for multiple approvals for purchases that were planned as part of a capital project.

1. Marcie Verdin, "TVA Revamps Procurement Process," (Tennessee Valley Authority), *TMA Journal*, January–February 1999, pp. 39–40, at 40.

- Consents can be simplified to the appropriate level or a single sign-off. Multiple approvals are frequently required, but the secondary approvers do not have adequate knowledge to make a decision and rely on the prior authorization.
- After-the-fact audits using sampling can be used to ensure that guidelines are being appropriately followed, rather than requiring sign-offs on each purchase request.
- A database (e.g., using LotusNotes) can be established in which notes are entered on actions taken, to ensure that every person involved has an understanding of the status of a purchase. These data can be integrated into a comprehensive purchasing/payables system with vendor histories, amounts purchased, performance, and quality.

New Economy Purchasing

The new economy requires buying and selling companies to leverage the Internet to gain a closer alignment with customers and partners, and to take advantage of developing revenue opportunities. Management of the supply line is critical, since production can cease when an overcommitted supplier misses delivery dates or if a shortage of a raw material arises. "E-procurement" provides a large selection of available goods and services, and delivery times are shortened. Transaction costs are reduced through automation and the use of decision support techniques to identify opportunities to shorten the supply chain. Companies can build strategic supplier relationships and use aggregate buying to gain volume discounts from vendors.[2]

E-Procurement

Electronic procurement packages allow the reviewing of and ordering from suppliers' catalogs on-line. Buyers are able to make purchases from their computers through e-procurement, where preferred suppliers are displayed. Some advance purchasing systems have multiple supplier catalogs on their networks. At the same time,

2. See David N. Burt and Richard L. Pinkerton, *A Purchasing Manager's Guide to Strategic Proactive Procurement* (New York: AMACOM, 1996).

the number of vendors can be reduced from perhaps thousands to a few hundred.

Buyers are freed from paper pushing, and procurement specialists can shift their focus to such strategic initiatives as negotiating volume pricing discounts, finding new sources of supply, refining procurement specifications, and improving purchasing of such technological products as computers. The system tracks all transactions with each vendor, allowing purchasing managers to document total spending with a supplier.

The vendor network can be rationalized to integrated work processes with key suppliers. Inventory levels can be managed on the basis of sales data so that commodity items from warehouse stock are delivered just-in-time. Raw materials can be ordered from suppliers in quantities based on a season's production forecast. Once an order is shipped, the vendor forwards an electronic shipping notice. The system prompts the inventory system to create barcoding labels for the incoming raw materials. The labels indicate product type, storage location, vendor, and date of receipt. As incoming materials are received and scanned, information systems update inventory levels and vendor accounts payable balances.

Sophisticated technology allows the development of spend/ trend analyses to enable the monitoring of purchases and the compiling of the data necessary to negotiate volume discounts with preferred suppliers. Companies that use such systems typically centralize purchasing in a function managed by professional buyers, who are skilled in supply base management and negotiations. In addition, they integrate a technology-based purchasing strategy, including purchasing cards, on-line procurement software, e-commerce procurement packages, and Web buying hubs.

Buying Hubs

Buying hubs are Websites that consolidate the on-line catalogs of various vendors, usually of the same types of products. There are now some 400 of these e-commerce "exchanges" for business, offering various permutations of hubs, auctions, and catalogs.[3] Software agents search for specific "markers" across the Internet to shop for

---

3. Patricia B. Seybold, "Niches Bring Riches," *Business 2.0*, June 13, 2000, pp. 135–136.

the most attractive offerings that meet specific buying criteria. Solicitations entered in an e-commerce purchasing system result in vendors' bids to meet the buying company's requirements.[4] The extent of services offered varies and, in addition to provision of a marketplace for buyers and sellers, may include credit reviews and funds transfers.[5]

A recent hub was announced by General Motors, Ford Motor, DaimlerChrysler, and Toyota Motor, combining their on-line purchasing to leverage the power of the $300+ billion a year they spend on parts and materials, in an attempt to win price concessions from suppliers and reduce costs by 10%.[6] The three U.S. automakers will create an on-line purchasing exchange that runs as an independent business and builds on separate exchanges previously formed by Ford with selected technology partners.

In addition to materials purchasing, a hub will be able to convert foreign exchange, keep track of global export regulations, and convey customer special orders to suppliers. Even though the hub simplifies the process by reducing the number of exchanges where suppliers bid for business, this innovation may increase pressures on supplier margins. Other hubs will likely develop for fragmented industries with geographically dispersed buyers and sellers. The choice of a hub depends largely on the function to be performed: will you be bartering, reviewing bids, or finding new suppliers?[7]

Accounts Payable

Payables functions confront piles of paper and procedures as they struggle to review P.O.'s, receive reports and invoices, and, upon

4. See Stewart McKie, "Crossing the Chasm," *Business Finance*, January 2000, pp. 67–70.
5. Selected hubs include Ariba Network, FreeMarkets, works.com, EDS CoNext, TradeOut.com, Ventro, Mercata, rfpMarket.com, and SupplierMarket.com. Hubs also specialize in particular industries, including chemicals, metals, paper, electronics, utilities, and energy.
6. Keith Bradsher, "Carmakers to Buy Parts on Internet," *New York Times*, February 26, 2000, pp. A1, C14. Toyota joined slightly after the first three; "Oh, What a Feeling: B2B," *Business Week*, May 15, 2000, p. 14. A hub for aerospace companies was announced shortly afterward, involving Boeing, BAE Systems, Raytheon, and Lockheed Martin.
7. See, Eric Krell, "The Hubbub over Web Hubs," Purchasing Supplement to *Business Finance*, March 2000, pp. 13–16.

approval, request the issuance of disbursements. Some companies do not attempt to actively manage the payables function and merely pay bills as presented if the necessary authorizations and accounting codes are provided and supporting documentation is attached. There is minimal concern for the appropriateness of the expense, for the value of float, or for variances among vendors as to their need for timely payment. In fact, payments may be made prior to the due date if a formal "diarying" system does not exist.

Other companies actively manage payables and attempt to maximize float and vendor relations. Management decisions are made regarding the importance of each counterparty, and triggers in the payables system enable taking cash discounts or paying on designated dates after invoice receipt. These "pay fast/pay slow" alternatives have required accounts payable managers to emerge from their clerical function of paying invoices as presented and reviewed to managing the process against such constraints as vendor sensitivity and the time value of money.

Regardless of the approach chosen by individual companies in managing payables, many now use integrated purchasing/payables systems. These products offer various analytical routines, controls on buying and paying decisions, restrictions on access to approved vendor lists, single file maintenance of all relevant vendor data, and interfaces with ACH and check disbursement systems. Later generations of purchasing/payables systems are integrated with various business applications and are now known as ERP (enterprise resource planning) systems; see the appendix to Chapter 12.

Outsourcing of Payables Functions

The outsourcing of the auditing of freight bills and payment issuance may be cost-effective for companies with limited financial and/or personnel resources.

Freight Bills

The management of freight bills can be outsourced to specialists that offer comprehensive logistics services. Transportation and distribution system can be designed to eliminate both flow problems and excessive or incorrect charges from freight bills. Freight auditors typically use a rating system to review freight invoices for common excessive charges such as misclassifications, incorrect discount levels, incorrect mileage calculations, extension errors, and ancillary charge errors. Overcharge claims can be filed and tracked to receive any overpaid fees. Other services offered include rate negotiation, review of contracts, classification and routing assistance, customized transportation and distribution systems, carrier selection, and contract negotiations.

Payment Issuance

Banks now offer the complete outsourcing of disbursement processing once a determination has been made that payments are owed and due. The process typically involves the initiation of payment by a transmission of a file (in agreed-upon format) to the selected bank through a VAN (an electronic value-added network). Disbursements can normally be issued the day following receipt of the file but can also be entered in a diary until the release date chosen by the company. The disbursements are issued, and funding of the daily clearing amount is initiated by notification to the issuer of the outstanding debit. All cleared items are reconciled, and appropriate detail and summary and information are provided.

The entire process of payment issuance is managed by the bank, and the corporate customer merely advises on exceptions once the payment file is prepared. Payments are made in any format acceptable or desired by the recipient, including checks and electronic transactions, in several of the major currencies. Remittance advices are transmitted to the bank in an agreed-upon format, printed by the bank, and attached to the check. Logos, signatures, and other non-standard data can be printed on the check and remittance advice.

Process Metrics

The following metrics are useful in determining sub-optimal processes in materials purchases:[8]

8. Process metrics are identified by chapter and item number and are summarized in the afterword to Part II along with a sequence number.

• 6-1: *Materials Utilization*. The most aggressive companies hold relatively small amounts of materials in their own inventory before the start of manufacturing and depend instead on their suppliers for just-in-time delivery. Tracking the trend of holding-period days for raw materials and purchased components can highlight excess materials purchased, which forces the commitment of working capital resources. In addition, the percentage of space (to total warehouse space) utilized for raw materials and purchased components should be used as an indicator of excess material carried in inventory. These metrics determine the efficiency of material requirements, scheduling, and expediting.

• 6-2: *Vendor Errors*. Mistakes by suppliers are usually resolved from data in P.O.s and receiving reports as matched against invoices. However, companies typically do not keep detailed records of such errors (except as remembered ''history''). It is useful to record the percentage of material shortages, overages, and below-specified-quality standards, as well as the items in error, particularly as these occurrences may adversely affect production schedules or result in excess inventory. These metrics can be useful in evaluating the performance of current suppliers when new P.O.'s are being negotiated.

• 6-3: *Materials Movement Time*. An important manufacturing metric is the period required to move materials to production, as measured over time. Any deterioration in this measure should be investigated to determine whether there are vertical or horizontal movement obstacles that can delay production scheduling, or whether are problems in developing or delivering instructions for pulling material from storage.

• 6-4: *Commodity Analysis.* The cost of many raw materials used in a production cycle can be hedged using publicly traded commodities contracts or options. A useful measure in determining price volatility is the ratio of the expected purchase price to the actual purchase price, plotted over time. The hedging utilization metric tracks the percentage of purchases hedged compared to total purchased dollars. Materials that cannot be protected by hedging contracts may be managed by long-term contracts with pricing guarantees.

• 6-5: *Expedited Purchasing*. The bureaucracy of purchasing approvals often results in a redundant, time-consuming, and costly administrative effort. Various actions have been noted in this chapter that can expedite buying decisions. An important metric is the total purchasing cycle time, from submission of a purchase request to the transmittal to the vendor, measured over time. The specific actions to shorten the cycle will vary by organization; what is important is that those actions be taken and that the old economy rules be reconsidered.

• 6-6: *Completion of Purchase Order/Receiver File*. A corollary metric is the completion of the purchase order/receiver file where required. We have noted that many companies permit the bypassing of established purchasing procedures. A particular problem is the failure to follow P.O. requirements or to complete receiving reports prior to authorizing payments to vendors. This metric determines the percentage of complete files for purchases that require these documents.

• 6-7: *Local Purchasing*. While there can be abuses associated with local procurement, there is considerable potential for a cost-effective, empowering activity that reduces the time and effort of central purchasing. Furthermore, companies that have implemented such initiatives as the use of purchasing cards have generally reported positive results in controlling local buying decisions. A process metric in evaluating these or similar efforts (e.g., the use of buying hubs) is the amount of participation by authorized employees. This measure requires an evaluation of the extent of the previous activity at the time the new procedure is activated, that is, how much local purchasing was occurring as a percentage of total procurement activity when the purchasing card program began.

• 6-8: *Issuance of Accounts Payable Remittances*. Accounts payable are often poorly monitored against predetermined target payment dates, such as the cash discount date, the due date, or some number of days after the due date as decided by management. This metric calculates the number of days prior to (as a negative number) or after (as a positive number) the target payment date that payments are issued. Details by the mechanism (e.g., checks, ACH, purchasing card) allow trend analysis on each payment mechanism.

• 6-9: *Cash Discounts Taken*. Any cash discount that is offered by vendors on terms of 1.5% (i.e., 1.5/10, net 30) or better (i.e., 2/10, net 30) should be taken, assuming an average corporate cost of capital. These discounts are usually missed because of a bureaucratic payables function or incomplete purchasing file data. A useful metric is the percentage of cash discounts taken when available as an indication of an efficient and financially aware organization. Cash discounts should not be taken after the stated period has expired, as doing so may harm vendor relations.

Gyzmo III

As discussed in Chapter 5, Smart's team discovered that raw materials were being purchased in anticipation of pricing increases or commodity shortages. Partnering with suppliers and instituting just-in-time procedures provided significant benefits by reducing idle materials stocks. The first step in this effort was to analyze Gyzmo's purchasing and payables activities, which were managed at each manufacturing site.

Purchasing Practices

Selection of vendors was made by the local production superintendent, with advice from his or her managers or supervisors. Maintenance of local vendor relations was considered important to ensure delivery of critical supplies and for community relations. Smart's analysts did note that several appointments with local production decision-makers were postponed due to vendor lunches and a few golf games. Selected activity is listed in Exhibit 6-2.

Smart requested that any available data on prices paid for the various items purchased be accumulated. However, none of the sites maintained such data, and they could not provide any statistics on quantities purchased, pricing discounts, or net prices paid. As a result, it was decided to pull vendor invoices for a three-month period on 50 significant materials, as summarized in Exhibit 6-3. It was discovered that the average price paid was substantially above fair market and that the range of prices (as measured by the standard deviation) was significant. It became quite obvious that local purchasing was inefficient, redundant, and expensive.

Accounts Payable Practices

A review was also conducted of the accounts payable function at each site. Payables disbursements were being made by check, using a variety of accounting software systems, with two major payables

Exhibit 6-2. Activity of selected large vendors.
(Assume that all invoices are received on the first of the month.)

	Terms	Typical Payment Date	Annual Payments ($ millions)	Value of 1 Day (at 9.37%)
TOOLS AND COMPONENTS				
Dodo Distribution	net 30	25th	$9.50	$3,561
Platypus Parts	net 20	25th	$6.89	$2,582
Unicorn Units	1/10, n/30	25th	$5.59	$2,095
Aardvark Aspects	net 25	25th	$4.82	$1,807
Windblown Answers	net 20	10th	$3.40	$1,274
Gone Flowers	net 30	10th	$1.78	$667
Rusty Diamonds	2/10, n/30	10th	$1.33	$498
Ringing Hammers	net 30	10th	$1.00	$375
Subtotal			$34.31	$12,859
PROCESS/ENVIRONMENTAL CONTROLS				
Windsor Works	net 30	25th	$20.50	$7,683
Avon Appliances	net 30	25th	$7.80	$2,923
Globe Global	net 30	25th	$5.67	$2,125
Falstaff Foundry	net 30	25th	$3.45	$1,293
Benny's Jacks	net 30	10th	$2.75	$1,031
Milton's Machines	net 30	10th	$1.87	$701
Red's Buttons	net 30	10th	$1.60	$600
Smothers' Sisters	net 30	10th	$1.00	$375
Subtotal			$44.64	$16,731
Total			$78.95	$29,590
Savings by payment on the due date*				$185,000

*The potential savings is the number of days invoices are paid early, times the value of one day's float. The calculation for this amount is as follows: Dodo Distribution (5 days)($3,561) + Unicorn Units (5)($2,095) + Windblown Answers (10)($1,274) + Gone Flowers (20)($667) + Ringing Hammers (20)($375) + Windsor Works (5)($7,683) + Avon Appliances (5)($2,923) + Globe Global (5)($2,125) + Falstaff Foundry (5)($1,293) + Benny's Jacks (20)($1,031) + Milton's Machines (20)($701) + Red's Buttons (20)($600) + Smothers' Brothers (20)($375) = $185,000/year. (No calculation is made for Rusty Diamonds as it is assumed that the 2% cash discount is taken.)

Exhibit 6-3. Statistics on Gyzmo raw materials purchases.

Material	Unit	Fair Market Price	Average Price	Standard Deviation	Number of Purchases
Steel	Ton	$125	$175	$30	38
Aluminum	Lb.	$1	$1.25	25¢	25
Copper	Plate	$100	$120	$15	37
Platinum	Oz.	$570	$600	$75	28
Fuel oil	Gallon	$.775	$.85	$.20	60
Lumber	1000 board ft.	$350	$400	$50	45

runs on the 10th and 25th of each month. The clerk handling payables at each site was also responsible for preparing all checks. Payables checks were signed by that clerk unless they exceeded $2,500, in which case the production superintendent was required to sign.

Gyzmo's payables disbursement system produced a total of 6,000 checks per month. The all-in cost of these checks is detailed in Exhibit 6-4. Various ideas had been suggested by the company's bankers and outside auditors to make the disbursement system more efficient, including analyzing computer requirements to reduce computer time and support; re-negotiating bank disbursement costs following competitive bidding; and outsourcing most disbursement activities to a bank and/or vendor.

Smart's Observations

After carefully documenting the requirements of each Gyzmo site, Smart's team presented its findings to senior management on centralizing all purchasing and payables. It was expected that consolidating these activities would lead to various efficiencies.

• *Purchasing.* Purchasing would be based on total Gyzmo requirements and managed by professionals. In addition to EOQ (economic order quantity) decision-rules and competitive bidding, price movements of certain raw materials could be hedged in the commodities markets.

Exhibit 6-4. GAGM payables disbursement costs.

LABOR	Hours/Yr.	Cost/Hr.	Annual Cost
Purchasing	800	$35	$28,000
Material handling	1000	$20	$20,000
Costs & budgets	600	$30	$18,000
Computer processing	1600	$35	$56,000
Computer printer	1000	$30	$30,000
Bursting & signing	600	$20	$12,000
Cash disbursements	800	$30	$24,000
Folding	1200	$20	$24,000
Stuffing	600	$20	$12,000
Mail operations	1200	$25	$30,000
Report preparation	1000	$45	$45,000
Management	1600	$60	$96,000
Total labor			$395,000

MATERIALS & BANKING	Volume/Yr.	Cost/Item	Annual Cost
Check stock	72,000	$0.175	$12,600
Envelopes	72,000	$0.075	$5,400
Printer supplies			$1,000
Bank charges	72,000	$0.625	$45,000
Total materials			$64,000

FIXED COSTS	Usage*	Fixed Cost	Annual Cost
Printer	8	$500	$4,000
Folding equipment	3	$750	$2,250
Stuffing equipment	3	$750	$2,250
Software support	6	$7,500	$45,000

Postage meters	8	$200	$1,600
Computer charge	350	$75	$26,250
Imputed rent	1000	$20	$20,000
Allocated sr. mgt. overhead		$35,000	$35,000
Total fixed costs			$136,350
Total costs			$595,350
Explicit cost per disbursement			$8.26
Postage savings from presorting**			$0.04
TOTAL COST PER DISBURSEMENT			$8.30

*No. of pieces of Gyzmo equipment or resources used each year.
**Difference between presort rate and full first-class postage.

• *Accounts Payable.* Local payables management caused early payment of invoices, some missed cash discounts, and failure to negotiate quantity purchase discounts. The value of payment on the due date is an annual $185,000; see Exhibit 6-2. Centralization would allow a consistent payables policy.

• *Control.* Because the same clerk was handling both cash and accounting functions, there is a control issue at each company site. The second signature requirement was not an adequate safeguard against fraud, since the clerk could issue checks to a phony vendor for any amount under $2,500.

• *Procurement Cards.* Gyzmo should consider use of a procurement card for designated managers for travel and entertainment expenses and for small purchases.

• *Outsourcing.* It might be feasible to outsource part or all of Gyzmo's disbursement activities. The company was paying considerably more than the typical price for disbursement services of 10–15¢, as the total costs of the present system were $8.30 per disbursement. As the charge by outsourcing companies (banks and vendors) is about 25–50 cents per item (exclusive of postage), the outsourcing savings on 6,000 items a month could be about $45,000 (more than $500,000/year). However, certain of the costs in Exhibit 6-4 might not be avoidable.

Although they disliked disturbing the autonomy of local managers, senior management had to agree with Smart that such corrective action was necessary. They also felt that investigation into e-commerce purchasing might develop savings by accessing a larger number of suppliers, reducing paperwork, and allowing various other efficiencies.

Chapter 7

WORK-IN-PROCESS

We might as reasonably dispute whether it is the upper or the under blade of a pair of scissors that cuts a piece of paper, as whether value is governed by utility or cost of production.

—Alfred Marshall (1842–1924),
Principles of Economics

Work-in-process (WIP) involves the assignment of the cost of materials, direct labor, and indirect manufacturing of goods that have started the production process but are not yet complete. Goods in WIP may be at varying stages in the production cycle at the time of the closing of accounting records, from entering a manufacturing process to nearly completely finished. Various concepts, briefly noted in the text, are described in more detail in the chapter appendix.

The costing of WIP requires an inspection of the goods in the manufacturing cycle and a determination of the approximate stage (or percentage) of completion, or the number of days of work completed or to be completed. Materials and direct labor are usually assigned directly to WIP. Indirect manufacturing costs must be assigned using a logical system of allocation, based on some measure of direct labor (i.e., hours or cost).

WIP Cycle Problems

It is critically important to carefully analyze WIP because of the inherent inefficiencies in most manufacturing situations. We have seen in the Gyzmo case that just-in-time and quality control efficiencies permitted a savings of five days (or about 15%). According to various observers, only a small portion of manufacturing cycle time is actually spent in making product,[1] with the remaining time spent in

1. Less than 5%, according to Brian H. Maskell, *Performance Measurement for World Class Manufacturing* (Portland, Ore.: Productivity Press, 1991), p. 124.

waiting, queuing, inspection, or other activities. These delays are compounded by changes in engineering specifications, order quantities, and manufacturing processes.

Long WIP cycles contribute to various accompanying problems. Among these are the following:

• *Increased Dependence on Forecasts.* Long WIP often necessitates increasing made-to-stock finished goods inventories to have products available for sale at the time of customer demand. This condition causes a dependence on sales forecasts, which are often unreliable, leading to unsold inventory, price markdowns, and additional costs.

• *Manufacturing Inflexibility.* Cycle time delays reduce a company's flexibility to alter production routines to meet nonstandard customer demands. While branded products (e.g., Gyzmo's T&C business segment) are usually not subject to unusual requirements, large systems nearly always have some unique configuration (e.g., Gyzmo's P/EC business segment). An important attribute of e-commerce manufacturing is the flexibility to build to precise customer requirements.

• *Work Center Congestion.* Production loading is compounded by lengthy WIP cycles and often results in bottlenecks at specific manufacturing stations. The layout of a production facility assumes a flow between workstations that may not function smoothly during long work cycles.

Managing WIP Cycles

WIP cycles can be shortened by having smaller lot sizes and by having synchronized production planning and control. Reducing the size of a manufacturing lot or group will lead to reduced cycle time but may affect economies of scale for overhead. The high cost of automated manufacturing and handling equipment necessitates calculation of economic order quantity (EOQ), derived from the costs to produce and hold finished goods inventory.

The old economy method of determining the costs of WIP is to convert inventories into finished equivalents (or equivalent units of production). This is calculated by multiplying the number of units times the stage of completion. For example, if 100 units were one-half completed, the finished equivalent would be 50 units. This process is flawed because it requires an estimation of the degree of the completion of production in order to assign costs. This essentially is a look at a process after the fact, rather than an accounting of the time involved in completing each stage in a production cycle.

The new economy approach to WIP avoids the judgment implicit in estimating the extent of completion by tracking work-days incurred once a WIP cycle begins. This can be accomplished in various ways:[2]

• *Detailed Recording of Cycle Times*. The capture of cycle data involves the recording of order numbers, product numbers, start and stop dates, waiting times in production queues, setup times, and physical movement. The use of bar coding technology or other automated data collection devices can expedite this effort. Bar codes are assigned to materials as they enter the production stream, and bar code readers can be used to monitor WIP progress.

• *Sampling of Cycle Times*. Rather than conducting a census of all items entering WIP, a statistical sample can be drawn to reduce the burden and expense of data collection. A scientifically drawn, stratified sample yields accurate results when relevant elements of the WIP population are adequately depicted. Various measures (such as the standard error, measuring the sample standard deviation) can be used to verify the representativeness of the sample compared to known census factors.

• *Analysis of Engineering Routing*. Rather than examine WIP items, engineering routing can be evaluated to determine cycle times. However, this approach assumes that such documentation is accurate and current, which is unlikely in most situations, given the frequent changes in many manufacturing processes.

WIP Cost Elements

The specific cost elements that offer opportunities for the calculation of process metrics include the setup of manufacturing activities; in-

2. Maskell, pp. 129–141. See also William Duncan, *Manufacturing 2000* (New York: AMACOM, 1994).

spection of work-in-process; scrap, spoilage and re-work; and pay-roll.

Manufacturing Setup

In the old economy, conventional standard-cost accounting measures calculate machine and employee utilization and treat in-process inventories as an asset. In many production facilities, it is extremely expensive to institute a manufacturing changeover. The strategy thought to be the most economical is mass production and long production runs with centralized control. As an alternative approach, some producers acquire equipment that can produce different products by simply changing part fabrication tools.

In the new economy, management's strategy is to foster flexible and customized production with decentralized control. The goal is to reduce setup time and smooth the production schedule on the basis of customer demands. Using these techniques, companies seek to eliminate the shutdown of an entire production process.

Inspection of WIP

In the old economy, inspection is conducted by a quality control group with little intervention from the production team unless a problem arises. Typically, a reactive quality control function samples the work being processed at different stages independent of the production line. Little feedback is given to production unless a problem arises. If there is a malfunction, the manufacturing line is halted and WIP is reworked to meet the target quality goal. Customers visit a production facility only if the product they receive has an unacceptable level of defects.

In the new economy, inspection and related tests are proactive and are typically performed at the supplier's site prior to shipment. Testing results are electronically transmitted directly to the customer. The customer then authorizes the shipment once inspection results are reviewed and accepted. The focus becomes the ''real time'' interchange of manufacturing inspection data and customer response, rather than building in cycle delays, failures, and the necessity for re-work.

Scrap, Spoilage, and Re-work

Even after taking significant measures to improve quality control, companies have some scrap, spoilage, and re-work.

- "Scrap" is the unwanted by-product of manufacture that has little sales value and may have negative value associated with removal costs. Accounting for the value of scrap is done at the time of production or at the time of sale, by recording the revenue in a separate line item, by offsetting overhead, or by charges against a specific job in WIP control.
- "Spoilage" is production that is no longer acceptable for regular sale and is to be discarded or sold for disposal value.
- "Re-work" includes goods that are defective or unacceptable either as quality control rejects or because of their failure to meet the needs and expectations of the buyer. Such goods may be re-worked and sold as acceptable finished goods through regular marketing or alternative channels.

In the old economy, normal spoilage occurs even in efficient production and is an inherent result of a manufacturing process. The expenses of such spoilage are considered part of the cost of goods produced and therefore treated as an inventory cost. Abnormal spoilage is not reasonably expected to occur under efficient operating conditions. Consistent with financial accounting theory, abnormal spoilage is accountable as a period cost.

Companies that have invested in just-in-time (JIT) and computer-integrated manufacturing systems justify the cost of these systems by the reduction in scrap, spoilage, and re-work. With improved quality and intolerance for high spoilage in the new economy, these organizations have increased sales and lowered overall costs. The new economy adheres to a perfection standard (e.g., "Six Sigma") as a part of the emphasis on total quality control. As a result, all spoilage, re-work, and scrap are treated as abnormal and accountable as a period cost.

In the old economy, some practices that inevitably led to errors and rework were accepted. The emphasis in the new economy on first time quality does not allow for these old practices. For example, old economy companies often positioned junior designers at the front end of a project while seasoned designers spearheaded urgent matters, leading to errors and rework. In the new economy, the sales force consists of experienced engineers equipped with design tools and the ability to quote jobs at the sales call visit. This practice reduces design time and eliminates the need for rework.

Payroll

Payroll checks are the dominant mechanism for pay, although "direct deposit" through the ACH to the employee's bank account has come into prominence. Direct deposit requires the employee to submit a voided copy of his or her bank account check to the employer, and various data from that check are used to credit that account on payday. These data include the transit routing number (the bank's digitized address) and the employee's bank account number.

A primary advantage to the employer of direct deposit is low cost; an ACH transaction costs about 10 cents, compared to the cost of a payroll check, generally estimated to be in excess of $1. Secondary benefits are reduced employee absence during the workday, as there is no need to leave the premises to deposit or cash the payroll check; and minimized account reconciliation of clearing items (except for those ACHs that "bounce" at closed employee checking accounts). A major disadvantage is the loss of float from the electronic transfer of funds, as the employer is debited at the same time that the employee is credited on payday. Studies show that the float loss is about equivalent to the lower cost of direct deposit.

Although certain areas of the U.S. (such as California) have successfully promoted the extensive use of direct deposit, many companies report the use of this mechanism at well below one-half of all pays. The usual reasons for employee reluctance to enroll in direct deposit are lack of a bank account, desire to hide pay from a spouse or friend, or simply lack of knowledge about the mechanics of the program. Aggressive promotion, assisted by bank marketing materials, usually results in significant employee participation.

Process Metrics

The following metrics are useful in determining sub-optimal processes in work-in-process:

• 7-1: *Direct Labor Expended*. It is essential to measure direct labor costs in contrast to other manufacturing parameters. Days of direct labor should be calculated by major product grouping, plant location, or other useful categorization. Statistics on direct hours from time cards or other primary data should be developed to determine the amount of standard time as compared to overtime, and idle time as compared to actual production time.

• 7-2: *Payroll Mechanisms*. The use of direct deposit simplifies the administration of payroll and reduces idle time when employees leave the premises to cash their checks. The use of each payment mechanism should be charted, and actions should be instituted to encourage direct deposit in situations of low usage (e.g., when usage is less than 75% of all "pays").

• 7-3: *Damage in Movement*. Materials can be damaged in movement at any point in manufacturing. Careful handling is essential to minimize destruction, re-work, and scrap. Metrics should be maintained on such damage to determine whether adequate care is being exercised. Such measures include: percent of materials damaged prior to production; number of re-work orders compared to production orders; and percentage of materials scrapped compared to the percentage entered into production.

• 7-4: *Assembly Line or Machinery Downtime*. Production downtime may result from scheduled maintenance, staffing adjustments, insufficient materials or WIP, machinery repairs, or other causes. It is important to chart the percentage of downtime to total manufacturing time to determine the trend of such inactivity and to investigate the cause of deterioration.

• 7-5: *Number of Inspection Failures Requiring Remedial Action*. During the quality control process there inevitably will be defects, flaws, and other problems requiring remedial action. In some cases, the product can be re-worked; in other situations, the damaged item will have to be scrapped. It is important to compare the number of fails requiring remedial action to the total number of items produced to develop a pattern of failures. The underlying causes should then be determined, such as faulty raw materials, problems in the production line, or mistakes in engineering design.

• 7-6: *Target versus Actual WIP*. Target WIP days include all of the production issues discussed throughout this chapter and is usually based on experience with the delivery of materials to the job site, an estimation of direct labor requirements, reworks, spoilage, and other factors. Actual WIP may vary significantly from these estimates, and variances should be measured in days and investigated to determine and correct the cause(s).

• 7-7: *Finished Goods Inventory Days-Equivalent*. The production of goods to be sold from stock is the predominant form of manufacturing. While it is obviously necessary to hold such inventory, working capital may be unduly obligated unless such production is carefully monitored. The standard ratio used in this measurement is "inventory turnover," defined as sales divided by inventories valued at the selling price, or cost of goods sold divided by inventory valued at cost. As inventories may fluctuate due to seasonal patterns, it is appropriate to use average inventories. A second but significant problem is that financial calculations tend to lump all inventories together, whereas a days-equivalent measure can be established for each product line.

• 7-8: *Finished Goods Shipped by Premium Carrier*. Promises made to customers in the course of a sales effort may be based on reasonable manufacturing expectations or can result from too aggressive efforts to close a deal. A useful metric to determine the extent of coordination between sales and production is to compare the number of items shipped to customers by premium carrier to the total number of items shipped (including truck and rail freight). A high level of premium carrier movements may indicate production bottlenecks and the inevitable costly efforts to meet customers' on-time delivery expectations.

• 7-9: *Timely Receipt of Progress Payments*. The sale of large systems often requires down payments and progress payments at specified points in the production cycle. These payments may be waived or delayed by salespeople or because of administrative oversight. It is important to develop a monitoring system to ensure the timely collection of these amounts, and lags should be measured as days of progress payment delay.

Gyzmo IV

Smart's review indicated significant variations in work-day requirements to inspect work-in-process, complete repair work, and revise the production schedule due to defects. Engineering studies would have to be conducted to determine whether these production quality concerns were related to worker training, plant layout and equipment, workflow, and/or manufacturing processes. However, it was apparent that the delays caused the deferral of large system shipment and customer acceptance, and explained in part the loose enforcement of progress payment requirements (noted in Chapter 4).

WIP Progress Payments

Smart decided to construct three months of selected large system payment history, shown in Exhibit 7-1.

It was apparent from the data that there was some loose enforcement of down payment and progress payment rules and that the impact on the large system targets were significant: the down payments for P/EC were coming in at 16.8%, instead of at the goal of 20%, while those for Squeaky Wheel were coming in at 27.4% instead of the target 30%. The gross value of the missed down payments (until the subsequent receipt of later customer payments) was $6.40 million for P/EC and $4.55 million for Squeaky Wheel.[3] The net value, based on some three months of average manufacturing and billing cycle time, would be $2.8 million.[4] These amounts were clearly unacceptable and required remedial action.

Payroll

In the course of reviewing labor costs, Smart's team examined the process of managing weekly payroll. Workers traditionally were paid by checks drawn on local banks, with the payroll envelopes distributed on Fridays just before lunch. The payables clerk at each site maintained cash in a strongbox for employees who wished to cash their payroll checks. An average of $20,000 was maintained at

3. Calculated as P/EC revenue of $200 million subject to down and progress payments times 3.2%, and Squeaky Wheel revenue of $175 million subject to down and progress payments times 2.6%.
4. Derived from Exhibit 4-6 data, with 93 days of manufacturing and billing time (the time to the shipment date) divided by 365 days, times $10.95 million ($6.4 million for P/EC and $4.55 million for Squeaky Wheel).

Exhibit 7-1. Gyzmo large system progress payment history.

	Sale Amount	Target Down	Actual Down*	Target at Shipment	Actual at Shipment*	Target at Acceptance	Actual Acceptance*
P/EC		20.0%	16.8%	70.0%	71.1%	10.0%	12.1%
Ludwig's Lizards	$1,000,000	$ 200,000	$ 100,000	$ 700,000	$ 800,000	$100,000	$100,000
Wolfgang's Wombats	$ 750,000	$ 150,000	$ 150,000	$ 525,000	$ 500,000	$ 75,000	$100,000
Igor's Iguanas	$ 600,000	$ 120,000	$ 120,000	$ 420,000	$ 400,000	$ 60,000	$ 80,000
Papa's Pests	$ 300,000	$ 60,000	$ 50,000	$ 210,000	$ 200,000	$ 30,000	$ 50,000
Giacomo's Giraffes	$ 500,000	$ 100,000	$ 100,000	$ 350,000	$ 350,000	$ 50,000	$ 50,000
Anton's Antelopes	$ 400,000	$ 80,000	$ 75,000	$ 280,000	$ 275,000	$ 40,000	$ 50,000
	$3,550,000	$ 710,000	$ 595,000	$2,485,000	$2,525,000	$355,000	$430,000
T&C: Squeaky Wheel		30.0%	27.4%	60.0%	55.8%	10.0%	16.8%
Bella's Boats	$ 650,000	$ 195,000	$ 175,000	$ 390,000	$ 350,000	$ 65,000	$125,000
Aircraft of Antonin	$ 800,000	$ 240,000	$ 200,000	$ 480,000	$ 450,000	$ 80,000	$150,000
Edward's Electric Trains	$1,200,000	$ 360,000	$ 350,000	$ 720,000	$ 700,000	$120,000	$150,000
Bach's Buses	$ 350,000	$ 105,000	$ 100,000	$ 210,000	$ 200,000	$ 35,000	$ 50,000
Carl's Cars	$ 700,000	$ 210,000	$ 200,000	$ 420,000	$ 400,000	$ 70,000	$100,000
Ships from Sergei	$1,500,000	$ 450,000	$ 400,000	$ 900,000	$ 800,000	$150,000	$300,000
	$5,200,000	$1,365,000	$1,425,000	$2,730,000	$2,900,000	$520,000	$875,000

*Actual percentages are dollar-weighted

each site (and at the home office) for this purpose; the funds were replenished by a check cashed by that clerk at the local bank.

Smart realized that there were several concerns with current payroll procedures. These included the following:

• *Imprest Balances*. Maintaining an imprest cash balance at each site invites theft and costs the company in lost float resulting from holding idle funds at each site to cash employee paychecks. In addition, banks charge for providing coin and currency services. There were occasional shortages when the strongbox was reconciled against accounting records, but these discrepancies had always been written off.

• *Direct Deposit*. The issuing of payroll checks off local banks misses the opportunity to direct-deposit pay through the banking system's ACH (Automated Clearinghouse). Direct deposit is a convenience for employees, eliminates the need for them to run to their banks during work hours (the parking lots were always empty on paydays), and is considerably less expensive than issuing and reconciling checks and holding imprest cash.

• *Paper Checks*. If checks are the preferred method of payment for certain employees, a single account could be used for all payroll to maximize float (the time for checks to be deposited and clear) and to simplify account management.

The annual savings achieved by implementing these changes in the administration of Gyzmo's payroll was valued at $60,000; see Exhibit 7-2.

Plant Sites and Costs

Smart realized that work-in-process delays could be improved but not corrected completely through just-in-time and quality control practices; see the discussion in Chapter 5. The situation at Lean Green Machine would probably not be resolved until a modern, single-story manufacturing facility was located. Other capital demands precluded a commitment to plant construction, although the need for expansion continued, possibly to a site in Texas or in Tennessee. The engineering complexities of Lean Green products made any decision difficult because of the requirement for a skilled, experienced workforce.

Senior management was considering an appropriate course of

Exhibit 7-2. Calculation of Gyzmo payroll cost savings.

Payroll Opportunity	*Site Cost Calculation*	*Total Savings (8 sites)*
Imprest cash	$20,000 @ 9.37%	$15,000
Coin and currency	$25/week	$10,000
Cash shortages	Estimated from accounting records	$5,000
Payroll checks Issuance/reconciliation		$65,000*
Less: Lost float		− $22,000
Less: Direct deposit		− $13,000**
Net payroll checks		$30,000
Total savings		$60,000

*2500 employees × 52 weeks × $1/check × 50% conversion to direct deposit.
**2500 employees × 52 weeks × 20¢/check × 50% conversion to direct deposit.

action when one of Smart's team observed that there were several Websites promoting economic development for their states.[5] For example, one state with excellent success in attracting business offered corporate income tax credits for initiatives such as job creation by a manufacturing company, a designated level of capital investment, or company-provided basic skills education and retraining programs. In addition, incentives from that state included one-stop environmental permitting; site location assistance; a training program including developing instructional materials and paying trainers' salaries, all at no expense to the company; and university-level technology support.

In discussing various alternatives, Smart began to realize that the current Gyzmo locations were chosen rather haphazardly and without much consideration for suitable company practice (see Exhibit 7-3). While it would be unreasonable to make numerous changes to current manufacturing sites, a review of WIP operations could provide significant benefits. Smart's team investigated Gyz-

5. For a list of and hyperlinks to state economic development Websites, see www.aggregatemarket.com/state-development.htm.

Exhibit 7-3. Gyzmo current and prospective location labor costs.

Gyzmo Locations	Average Pay	Pay as % of U.S. Average
Average for U.S. cities	$33,381	
Springfield, Missouri	$24,743	74.1%
Baltimore, Maryland	$32,752	98.1%
Fresno, California	$23,822	71.4%
Hartford, Connecticut	$38,504	115.3%
Jacksonville, Florida	$29,937	89.7%
St. Paul, Minnesota	$35,626	106.7%
Average for U.S. states	$31,908	
Tennessee	$28,457	89.2%
Texas	$31,512	98.8%

Source: U.S. Department of Labor Website, www.stats.bls.gov.

mo's various current and prospective locations and realized that Gyzmo's labor costs were seriously impacted by competition for skilled workers in certain locations, particularly Hartford and St. Paul. Any decision to expand manufacturing facilities should include consideration of labor costs along with economic development support.

A financial analysis of the difference between the labor costs in St. Paul and in Tennessee showed a potential annual savings of $2 million.[6] A new facility would offer the opportunity to minimize workflow bottlenecks to reduce work-day delays. This realization caused Smart to suggest possibly moving the 250-person St. Paul operation to a new site and motivated the senior management team to begin to seriously investigate the various attractions and incentives offered by Tennessee, Texas, and other state governments.

6. This calculation is based on the 250-person workforce times the difference in average pay ($35,626–$28,457), plus 15% of the difference for fringe benefits, as reduced by termination and staff and plant re-location costs. Various experts note that the cost of a business move is usually equivalent to the first year's savings.

MANUFACTURING/ SUPPLY CHAIN MANAGEMENT

Various "scientific" concepts have been developed over the past two decades to improve manufacturing efficiency. Supply chain management (SCM) attempts to optimize manufacturing, materials purchases, inventory management, and shipping.[7] Some of the key concepts in SCM are the following:

Just-in-Time (JIT). A manufacturing concept that eliminates waste, fosters quality, and continuously improves productivity. Production activities are planned and managed to maintain the minimum required inventory of materials, to achieve zero defects, to reduce setup and waiting times, and to control costs.

Economic Order Quantity (EOQ). A fixed-order-quantity model used to calculate manufacturing lot size (or components purchase), which optimizes the costs of producing and carrying inventory. The formula is:

Quantity = Square of (two times annual demand times
average cost of order preparation, divided by
the annual inventory carrying cost percentage
times the unit cost)

Kanban. A JIT method based on a pull system for the restocking of inventory. Workstations indicate by a signal with a card that parts

---

7. Numerous excellent texts on SCM are available, including David A. Riggs and Sharon L. Robbins, *The Executive's Guide to Supply Management Strategies* (New York: AMACOM, 1998); and Fred A. Kuglin and Barbara A. Rosenbaum, *The Supply Chain Network @ Internet Speed* (New York: AMACOM Books, 2000).

or supplies are needed, and standard containers or lot sizes are used for replenishment. Kanban is a loose Japanese translation for "card" or "sign"; the Toyota Corporation is generally given credit for the successful implementation of Kanban.

Material and Manufacturing Resource Planning. MRP constitutes a series of techniques to determine the optimal time and component requirements for manufacturing processes, including the bills of materials, inventory data, and the master production schedule. End product demand is analyzed to determine the structure of products, to enable the preparation of purchase orders and production schedules. The result is a reduction in inventory and production times and improved customer commitments. The concept has been expanded to the entire business plan, including objectives, sales and production planning, financial requirements, relevant support systems, and "what-if" alternatives (MRP II).

Six Sigma. A process management program intended to produce fewer than 3.4 defects per million opportunities for error. Close scrutiny of business operations allows the determination of errors and their causes, and the implementation of corrective actions. The program is credited with improving equipment usage, cycle times, and customer service inquiry responses, as well as reducing inspection, rework, scrap, and other manufacturing costs. Various benefit estimates have been made for Six Sigma, with the general consensus in the range of an annual 10 to 20%. The use of the term "sigma" is derived from the statistical use of *sigma* as the measure of standard deviation. Six sigma calculates the defects per million based on the number of standard deviations from the mean (average) result and is considered world-class performance.

TQM and ISO 9000. TQM ("total quality management") is a continuous process for managing quality involving an orientation to perpetual improvement. TQM activities include: meeting customer requirements; reducing development cycle time; implementing just-in-time (JIT)/demand flow manufacturing; using improvement teams; reducing product and service costs; and improving administrative systems training. TQM involves:

- Defining the process
- Measuring and reviewing process performance
- Identifying process shortcomings
- Analyzing process problems

- Making required process changes
- Measuring the effects of the process change

ISO 9000 is an international organization that certifies companies that attain superior manufacturing and process control; a revised version ISO 9001 containing customer satisfaction and measurement requirements is being implemented in 2000. ISO 9000/9001 organizations are required to meet some two dozen process and quality criteria. Companies awarded the designation are given preference in bidding on business and often avoid audits or inspections by customers, who can depend on the quality performance of their suppliers. Where an ISO system is in place, about 75% of the required TQM steps have been completed.

Chapter 8

INVOICE PREPARATION

Error i' th' bill, sir, error i' th' bill.

—William Shakespeare (1564–1616),
The Taming of the Shrew

The invoice generation cycle is a function without a manager. Many companies handle invoicing as an afterthought, without concern for the need to provide quality content to the customer as he or she considers whether, when, and how much to pay. E-commerce developments are changing these attitudes, with the invoicing cycle being carefully analyzed and considered for electronic processes.

Old Economy Invoicing

Assuming that an old economy company is organized by function[1], is invoicing a sales activity, an element in the production cycle, a financial task, or a systems responsibility? In practice, it's a bit of each of these business functions but the responsibility of no one. Some of the decisions in the invoicing cycle are described in the sections that follow.

Content

The "invoicing cycle" refers to the process of assembling data from manufacturing and other production areas; verifying the data; determining that the invoice is in compliance with purchase order, contractual, or other agreements; and producing and delivering the invoice to customers. Various delays may interfere with timely data gathering, including incomplete or inaccurate data input from the

1. See Chapter 1, pp. 16–17.

materials or work-in-process cycles; the complexity of billing arrangements, particularly for large systems contracts; and demands
on the limited time of customer service or billing personnel.

Business practice uses at least three different billing delivera-
bles: the invoice that accompanies or follows a shipment; a statement issued periodically (usually monthly) showing open or
unpaid customer purchases; and reminder notices to request payment when normal payment terms have not been met. The issuance
of such varying documents is confusing to customers and often con-
veys erroneous or conflicting data. Payments may have been made
that are not reflected on statements; reminder notices may be issued
although both parties have acknowledged that there is a legitimate
dispute, such as damaged or returned merchandise; and data on
each document may be incomplete as to the specifics of the reported
transactions.

Some companies even assign paid invoice processing to one
function (e.g., accounts receivable) and statement processing to a
separate function (e.g., credit and collections). These units may not
be in close communication with each other and often have conflicting objectives: Receivables wants to retain customer goodwill as
measured by satisfaction surveys; credit and collections to get past-
dues paid as measured by late accounts cleared.

Format

Invoice design and layout decisions are often made by graphics staff
with insufficient concern for the display of information critical to
the needs of customers' payables clerks. A seller's accounts payable
function must be able to match the seller's records to those of their
counter party, which requires data such as account number, dates,
product codes, descriptions, pricing, and price extensions. Furthermore, the established terms of sale must be indicated, including
cash discounts, payment dates, and contacts in case there is a need
to resolve a disagreement. Disputes may arise because the data provided are inadequate to allow the transaction to be properly identified.

Invoice design may involve developing formats that can be read
by automated equipment, including those in MICR and OCR fonts.
MICR (magnetic ink character recognition) and OCR (optical character recognition) are fonts or print characters that have distinctive

designs recognizable by reader-sorter equipment. MICR and OCR characters are printed in special ink and usually are placed at the bottom of the print page. (MICR and OCR are most often used in consumer applications where the payment amount is relatively small and consistent over time, such as for utility companies, insurers, or cable television.)

Timing

The invoice cycle "run" of computation and printing is often made at the convenience of systems managers. Invoice runs are frequently inserted in the mainframe computer processing cycle as time is available, without regard to the optimal timing of the printing/mailing process. Substantial research has been conducted over the past two decades by the author and by large mailers on the optimal timing for corporate and retail payments. These tests have examined alternative invoice mailing dates and the resulting payment "receive" date.

For most industries, the optimal time for the customer to receive the monthly statement is 25 days prior to the due date for receipt of funds on or near the date due. The presumption is that the recipient needs sufficient time to review and pay but not so much time that the bill can be "misplaced" or forgotten. The selling company wants to provide the buyer with a "current" statement, that is, with all paid charges deleted, to avoid unnecessary disputes leading to payment delays.

Systems scheduling or accounts receivables updating forces some companies to invoice 10 to 15 days later than optimal, with the result that their DSO (days sales outstanding) is longer than the average for their industry. (Equivalent relationships hold for invoices issued on cycles other than monthly.) For example, a statement issued representing open accounts as of the end of the month will not run until about the second or third business day of the next month. By the time the bill is reviewed, mailed, and received by the buying organization, it is about the seventh business day (usually the tenth calendar day).

The terms may be "net 30," but the customer does not even begin the process of review and payment until calendar day 11 or 12. There is little likelihood of payment within the stated terms, given these tight times. If a cash discount is offered, say "2/10, net

30,"[2] the customer will have already missed the presumed cash discount date of the tenth of the month. Despite this, the discount will likely be taken, possibly on or about day 21 or 22. As a result, the seller is out more than ten days of float each month.

Remittance Location

Multiple company locations may be printed on the invoice, confusing the payables function as to the correct mailing address: headquarters, the sales office, the regional office, or the lockbox? It is little wonder that many items are directed to the wrong location. The "remit to" address should be clearly indicated, with a telephone contact provided for questions or the resolution of disputed items but no second address.

Whether the customer's actions are innocent or intended, companies should follow up on chronically misdirected customer payments to determine the causes. Many companies experience delays from re-mails, yet do not bother to ascertain the factors driving the misdirects. For example, are customers deliberately using incorrect addresses to extend float? Is the address imbedded in a vendor file, requiring a "change request" initiated by a manager? Is the customer discarding the return envelope and misaddressing its own business envelopes? Aggressive actions by selling companies can significantly reduce mail float on collections, often valued in the hundreds of thousands of dollars.

Mail Times

The delivery of mail to the U.S. Postal Service is the final invoicing task over which the selling company has some control. Mail delivery

---

2. This means that a 2% cash discount may be taken if the bill is paid within 10 days of receipts; the total amount is due in 30 days. Such a discount is worth 36% to the buyer, calculated as the number of "full payment periods" in a year (18, from $360 \div [30-10]$) times the discount (2%). Between 10 and 20% of the invoices received by manufacturing companies offer terms other than net (no cash discount offered), including 1/10, net 30; 2/10, net 30; 2/20, net 30; and 0.5/10, net 30). Net 30 continues to dominate vendor terms, although some companies are beginning to bill on terms of net 15 and even net 10.

times vary by sending and receiving post offices and average about three calendar days nationwide. The optimal selection of the "send point" is critical in reducing mail time (or "mail float"). Long mail times can result from envelope hygiene problems, including poor ink quality, errors in addressing, addresses that appear outside the target field area, shifting of documents in window envelopes, and inappropriate envelope size.

Main city post offices consistently process more efficiently than suburban or rural facilities. For example, mail sent from Los Angeles requires about 2.5 days for delivery (to nationwide addresses), while mail sent from towns in the Los Angeles metropolitan area require about one-quarter of a day longer, and rural Southern California towns an additional one-half day. The location and precise time for optimal outgoing mail performance can be determined through discussions with the Postal Service or through studies of database mail times.

According to recent data compiled by Phoenix-Hecht,[3] about one-half of the postal sites surveyed experienced deterioration from the previous year's survey, averaging four hours. The cities with the fastest times continue to be Atlanta, Chicago, Los Angeles, Philadelphia, Pittsburgh, and St. Louis. In the coming years, the U.S. Postal Service is expected to migrate more mail to ground transportation from air cargo, slowing national mail times.

Old Economy Invoice Cycles

The old economy invoicing cycle (up to the payment of the remittance by the customer) can require nearly two months of elapsed time:[4]

Compilation of invoice data	3 days
Final invoice review	3 days

3. This organization, located in Research Triangle Park, North Carolina, is the leading provider of market research for the financial services industry. The data cited are from the 1999 postal survey, as discussed on the company's Website, www.phoenixhecht.com.
4. These estimates are based on our observations of the invoicing cycle of 250 corporate clients.

Invoice printing and mailing   1 day
Mail time   3 days
Customer processing[5]   45 days

Of course, invoicing for standard products can be accomplished by automated systems, requiring significantly less setup time. However, customer processing is not affected by actions of the seller.

New Economy Invoicing

E-commerce and reengineering initiatives have prompted significant developments in the invoicing cycle.

Electronic Invoicing

The drive to reduce paper transactions and to outsource non-core activities has stimulated the introduction of a new invoicing product, known generically as Electronic Bill Presentment and Payment (EBPP). Selling companies send a file to a bank or vendor each day containing open invoices, which are then posted to customer files for viewing, review, and payment over a secure Website. The customer clicks on a "pay bills" button, chooses which invoices to pay, and electronically instructs the intermediary to execute the payment.[6] Communications regarding disputed invoices are e-mailed to the seller and are researched and resolved. The bank or vendor notifies the selling company when payments are received so that the invoice can be deleted from receivables.

The obvious attraction of EBPP is the conversion of billing transactions from paper-based to electronic files. The process of mapping and inputting invoice and statement data is complicated by the variety of statistics in the typical corporate record. Another complication is the numerous ways in which customers process their bills. Businesses do not simply pay invoices as presented: there

---

5. Published statistics show that "days sales outstanding" (DSO) practice in the U.S. varies from about 30 to about 60 days, depending on the practice in specific industries. Average DSO is about 45 days; see Dun and Bradstreet or Robert Morris Associates reports.
6. Mechanisms for transferring funds are discussed in Chapter 9.

may be disputes, and multiple approvals or reviews may be required prior to payment.

Benefits from EBPP

The savings to the selling company relate to the cost of printing, handling, and mailing invoices, which we estimate at $1 to $2 per invoice. The potential benefit of the near elimination of cycle time is also substantial, although difficult to measure. Furthermore, all data are in a standardized electronic file format, allowing their application to receivables files without further keying or data management. The customer does not have to handle paper and can execute a payment without having to manage a paper-based accounts payable function. Eventually sellers and customers can have integrated accounting systems to allow seamless data movement between receivables and payables files.[7]

New economy companies are attempting to develop strategic alliances or partnerships with their counterparties. EBPP promotes this interaction by allowing the exchange of information in a nearly real-time environment and by encouraging each party to format electronic files to readily glean information that can improve the other's operations. The seller can discern customer buying patterns and other marketing data, can resolve disputes, and can develop special pricing, cash discounts, and offers of collateral products or other follow-up. The buyer can exchange views regarding product offerings, satisfaction or complaints, and other relevant communications.

New Economy Invoice Cycles

The adoption of EBPP or similar e-commerce invoicing applications offers the possibility of reducing the combined setup and mail time requirement to one to two days, from the old economy's 10 days. Significant collateral benefits include the partnering of buyers and sellers, encouraging improved data exchange and service; and the possibility of reducing the average 45-day customer processing pe-

7. According to various sources, banks that offer or are developing versions of this service include Bank of America, Northern Trust, PNC, First Union, Chase, and Mellon Bank.

riod. While there is limited experience with e-commerce invoicing, these closer working relationships are expected to ultimately impact DSO times.

Process Metrics

The following metrics are useful in determining sub-optimal processes in invoice preparation.

  • 8-1: *Pre-Invoice Preparation Time*. The time required to assemble, verify, and input data to prepare an invoice or statement can involve as much as one to two weeks, depending on the extent of automation, the number of assembly points, and the complexity of the governing purchase order. This element of the invoice preparation cycle should be carefully monitored and excessive times reviewed to introduce efficiencies.

  • 8-2: *Days of System Downtime That Cause Invoicing Delays*. Once all pre-invoice activity has been completed, the actual invoice run may be delayed by system downtime or unavailability. This metric is calculated as the date the invoice is actually sent compared to the date the pre-invoice preparation is completed and can suggest scheduling changes, alternative procedures, or outsourcing.

  • 8-3: *Invoicing after Optimal Date*. Invoicing 25 days prior to the due date is optimal for most companies. Your company should determine the optimal period by testing alternative mailing dates to customers. This can be accomplished through a series of tests using alternative lead times and observing the timing of customers' payment responses. (Few companies compile this information except for "past-dues" and have no idea when their good customers pay after the due date.) Once an optimal time is determined, the metric to track is the number of days after the optimal date that invoices are actually issued. Any slippage from optimal should be investigated to determine and correct the cause(s).

  • 8-4: *Days of Mail Delay*. The mailing of invoices from sender to receiver averages some three days, which can be measured either by reference to standard databases (e.g., Phoenix-Hecht), U.S. Postal Service scheduled times, or from a test mailing to receiving points in your customers' locations. There may be viable alternatives to your current procedures, such as printing and mailing at sites closer to your customers, possibly through outsourcing; and the use of Internet electronic billing.

   • 8-5: *Disputed Invoices Resolution Time*. Invoices may generate disputes arising from "short" shipments, returned items, pricing disputes, failures to properly credit previous payments, and problems of product quality. The time required to resolve these disputes can be measured and reviewed to determine whether there are correctable causal factors.

   • 8-6: *Number of Customer Service Contacts to Satisfy Invoice Disputes*. In addition to the time required to resolve disputes, the number of customer telephone or written communications can be recorded in a Lotus Notes–type database. Since repeated contacts can obviously exasperate customers, this metric should be carefully monitored.

Gyzmo V

Gyzmo has been reasonably effective in completing its billing cycle, which involves the assembly of data from various production work areas, the verification of the data, and the preparation of invoices. The average P/EC billing cycle time is 12 days. The outlier is Lean Green Machine at 15 days, largely because of the need to match draft invoices against contract requirements and limitations.

   Smart discovered that the billing cycle was actually managed by the Information Systems Group, which determined that invoices would be printed at its convenience, on every second Thursday at 3 A.M. This caused numerous delays in billing completed work and often resulted in up to a week's delay in the receipt of the invoice by the customer. Furthermore, any problems discovered at 3 A.M. could not be resolved until the next day (at the earliest), causing those invoices with errors to be held until the next billing run two weeks later. Revisions to the invoicing system could result in three days of reduced data collection and review times and the earlier generation of customer bills.

   As Smart discovered in his review of the invoicing cycle, the time to assemble data from work areas, verify data, match draft invoices against purchase orders, and create and mail invoices averages 12 days. Specific activities included in the invoicing cycle for large systems billing for P/EC and Squeaky Wheel (P&C) include:

Closing the work order and transmission of data	$2^1/_2$ days
Preparation of a draft invoice	$1^1/_2$ days
Review against purchase order or contract	3 days
Corrections to invoice	$1^1/_2$ days
Final printing and mailing	$4^1/_2$ days

Other T&C business segments operate on an assembly-line manufacturing basis, with production primarily for inventory. Those businesses do not require the initial two days of work order review and data transmittal, and their invoicing cycle therefore averages 11 days.

While cooperation with the Information Systems Group produced an average reduction of three days in the invoicing timeline, Smart believed that the cycle should be examined for other specific causes of delays. His team documented the relevant activities in each business segment, noting timing, data input, physical movement, clerical review, the matching of records and files, and the cause of errors. Bottlenecks result from the following factors (in order of occurrence).

1. *Manufacturing Data.* Incomplete or inaccurate data were input in production areas. Smart determined that data were manually key-entered at 10 different workstations for the typical large system. The responsibility for data entry belonged to the supervisor or foreman who was also managing the workstations' activity "loading," the assignment of workers to each project, overtime scheduling, the delivery of materials, and a variety of other activities. The supervisor often made errors due to time delays between the completion of the activity and the data entry, which often occurred at the conclusion of the work shift.

2. *Billing Arrangements.* Complex billing arrangements were common in the large systems businesses. There were various invoicing procedures that applied to particular systems, depending on the arrangements made at the time of the sale. Certain long-time customers had demanded cost-plus pricing, requiring detailed record-keeping for each expense incurred. Most customers agreed to a specific price for the system being purchased, with standard costs

used to price the various modules included and other components. A few customers had begun to request pricing based on a complete systems design, assembly, installation, periodic servicing, parts replacement, and the training of their staff.

3. *Demands on Billing Clerks.* Numerous demands were made on billing clerks. The clerical staff was expected to respond to customer questions, keep customers informed of the status of work, search for files containing purchase orders or other documents, and provide a full range of customer services. Clerks often set aside the preparation of invoices so that they could respond to customer inquiries. Because the invoicing system was not fully computerized, they had to conduct some research in files and records located in various Gyzmo work areas.

4. *Multiple Invoicing Systems.* Although the basic system used for all collection activity was OES, particular product and business segment needs that evolved over time resulted in the development of multiple invoicing procedures. Customer and Gyzmo staff were frequently confused by different invoices, statements, special bills, and reminders, resulting in errors by both parties.

5. *Manager Invoice Review.* Delays were also caused by the frequent absences of receivables managers who were required to review and confirm to draft large system invoices. These managers were frequently called into sales or manufacturing meetings, customer presentations, or general administrative reviews, and so were engaged in other critical activities. Furthermore, the complexity of billing systems made manager training lengthy and expensive, and management had effectively become captive to its demands for additional staff, better computers, and other resources.

As previously noted, the "standard product" business segments of Gyzmo had less complex invoicing requirements. However, the inefficiencies of the old OES system and its successors inevitably led to unnecessary billing delays and errors.

Gyzmo's New Invoicing System

Smart decided to restructure Gyzmo's invoicing system to more easily enter and maintain billing data. Rather than rely on data entry at manufacturing workstations, bar codes would be applied to purchased materials and during work-in-process so that scanners could capture the beginning and ending of each production task. Costs could then be applied on the basis of standards derived from a sample of recent history.

The billing process would be further simplified by eliminating customized invoicing. Quotes to customers would be based on established module prices and assembly, and cost-plus or other variations would be eliminated. Once the data were entered into the new order entry/receivables system (OES II), no further manipulation would be required to generate the invoice (although managers still had to review large system bills).

These changes were useful, but Smart understood that delays and costs would still be significant in a paper-based invoicing system. In the search for additional efficiencies, he wondered if the advantages of electronics could be applied to the transmittal of Gyzmo invoices without requiring a significant investment. Discussions with various e-commerce developers led to the realization that the company's Website, Gyzmo.com, could be used to deliver invoices electronically. Several systems integrators were capable of accepting an invoice file in a variety of formats, including flat files or in an EDI configuration[8], and mapping, translating, and loading the invoices for access by customers.

The conversion process could be handled entirely by a software company, which would receive Gyzmo's files through a VAN[9] transmission. In addition, customers could receive e-mail notification that an invoice has been "delivered," with amounts due, required payment dates, and other messages. Hyperlinks to Gyzmo's Website could be included to connect customers directly to the invoices. Once the bills were paid, the systems integrator could concentrate remittance data about payments in a file format compatible with Gyzmo's requirements for purposes of receivables posting.

Smart knew that there would be significant opportunities to save postage, printing, and handling costs by converting to electronic invoicing, in addition to the benefits from reduced work-days.

8. This involves the movement of business data electronically between companies in a structured computer-processable format. "Flat files" use company-specific formats that must be translated by the recipient for further manipulation and processing. "Electronic data interchange" (EDI) may include financial and non-financial data.
9. See Chapter 6, p. 132.

His team estimated that each paper bill cost the company $2, compared to 25 cents for each electronic invoice. Since Gyzmo issued 6,500 to 7,000 invoices every month, the conversion of one-half of the current customer base to an e-commerce format would save nearly $150,000 a year. In addition, customer service would be improved through on-line response to queries.

A discussion with the senior management team won its support for the idea of an e-commerce invoicing initiative. The traditional paper-based invoice process would continue to be available to customers, but the electronic format would be presented as an alternative. To induce customers to use the e-commerce alternative, a 1% cash discount would be offered if payment was received within 5 days of the invoice.

Chapter 9

RECEIPT OF GOOD FUNDS

In our wholly factitious society, to have no cash at all means frightful want or absolute powerlessness.

—George Sand (1804–1876),
Histoire de ma vie

The invoice has been mailed or an electronic file containing invoicing data has been sent through the EBPP system. You expect your customer to send a payment once your data are reviewed against receiving reports, purchase orders, and contract files. Depending on the form that payment will take and how it is handled, the process of receiving good funds can represent several days in the transaction cycle.

Old Economy Good Funds

The seller has various choices as to where to direct the buyer's remittances, depending on the dollar value of anticipated receipts, the willingness of customers to use electronic payment mechanisms, and the need for control over the receipts process. Smaller selling businesses generally ask that direct payments be sent to corporate offices (or post office boxes), where they process items received, prepare deposit tickets, bank customers' checks, and reconcile remittances against accounts receivable. Larger businesses use a bank product called a "lockbox."

Lockboxing

A lockbox is a collection mechanism that allows mail containing payments to by-pass corporate offices, going directly to a post office box maintained by the bank of deposit. The time or "float" required to process the check is reduced, because the bank can process items within hours and deposit the checks for clearing. After depositing checks, remittance advices, photocopies of the check, and other supporting material are forwarded to the company.

There are two basic types of lockboxing arrangements:

• *Wholesale Processing*. Basic invoice and check data are key entered at the bank, and check copies and original remittance documents are sent to the company for receivables processing.

• *Retail Processing*. Data are captured from encoded MICR and/or OCR information from the check and/or remittance documents and transmitted to the company in a data file.[1] This transmission is the primary input for receivables processing, although the remittance documents can be retained as supplementary confirmation.

An additional service available from banks (and some vendors) is the imaging of the remittance documents for receivables matching. "Imaging" involves taking an electronic picture of remittance documents, which can be archived, sorted, and processed according to a predetermined template. The imaged data can then be matched against open accounts receivable.

Check Clearing

Checks enter the U.S. clearing system at the time the depository bank begins its delivery to the drawee bank through any of several arrangements:

• *Direct Sends*. A cash letter (or package of checks) may be sent directly to the drawee bank to expedite delivery.

• *On-Us (or On-We)*. The check is deposited on the drawee bank ("on-us") or within the family of banks ("on-we") and clears by a charge to the payor's account and a credit to the payee's account.

• *Clearing Houses*. Within a geographic area, banks meet to exchange checks drawn on each other's accounts.

• *Federal Reserve*. The receiving bank deposits the checks it collects in an account at the Federal Reserve, which handles the checks' delivery to the drawee bank for clearing.

1. For an explanation of OCR and MICR, see Chapter 8, pp. 166–167.

The process of clearing (or "availability") involves up to two business days for commercial banks, and three days or more for other financial institutions. The specific time of clearing for each drawee bank is listed in an availability schedule by the depository bank.

Management of Collection Float

Collection float is the total of mail, processing, and availability time. The traditional procedure to minimize collection float has been the determination of the correct location and number of lockboxes. This decision is based on a float model that analyzes mail times, clearing times, and other factors to quantify the optimal lockbox configuration.[2] Usual outcomes are one or two lockboxes in the fastest processing cities[3] at recognized lockbox banks.

A lockboxing arrangement normally saves about two to three calendar days over in-house processing, worth more than $100,000 to a company processing an annual $500 million (at a 10% cost of capital) after deducting all lockbox costs. In addition, information is more quickly obtained about payments; the need for office staff and equipment for check processing is reduced; and the possibility of the theft of checks received at the office is eliminated. Other than the nuisance of managing a flow of paper, there are no significant disadvantages in the use of lockboxing.

Electronic Funds Transfer

Electronic funds transfer mechanisms are used for same-day and next-day transaction settlement. Same-day settlement is available through Fedwire and next-day through the ACH.[4] The use of these mechanisms is fairly limited, as there are now some 65–70 billion checks written each year, compared to only six billion ACHs and 100 million Fedwires. The U.S. is a particularly paper-intensive country in terms of payment settlement, and other countries have a much higher proportion of electronic funds usage.

ACHs are stored, batched, and sent at the end of the business

2. The leading provider of lockbox models and databases is Phoenix-Hecht; see Chapter 8, footnote 3, p. 169.
3. See Chapter 8, p. 169.
4. The ACH and Fedwire are defined in Chapter 2, footnote 22, p. 45.

day through a network of regional clearing houses and banks to the recipient. Access to terminal-based ACH processing, developed in recent years, will accelerate its use for corporate transactions. Fedwire is the funds transfer system of the Federal Reserve. Unlike ACH, Fedwires are real-time transactions between banks, with the Federal Reserve accounts of each institution debited and credited. The transaction is final and cannot be "bounced" or rejected, unlike checks and ACHs. The cost of Fedwire is about 100 times that of an ACH (about $10–$15 compared to 10–15 cents).

New Economy Good Funds

There is no real expectation of any rapid conversion from paper to electronic to settle business transactions. The most likely new economy initiatives are the continued merger of U.S. banks, leading eventually to lessened check clearing time; and the integration of the payment function into comprehensive e-commerce products to expedite the use of electronic payments. Each of these developments is discussed in the sections that follow.

Bank Mergers and Clearing Times

The McFadden Act of 1927 effectively prohibited interstate banking in the U.S., although the individual states could jointly approve branching across state lines. This legislation, designed to protect small-town and rural banks from urban competitors, resulted by the 1990s in a crazy-quilt pattern of some 15,000 commercial banks. In addition, there were an equivalent number of financial institutions that provided bank-like services, including credit unions, savings and loans, and savings banks. Although McFadden was phased out of existence beginning in 1997, nearly 10,000 commercial banks are still in business.

The significance of this situation is that depository banks have had to physically present the checks of drawee banks to accomplish clearing. (There has been limited migration to "electronic check presentment," which captures checks' MICR lines at the depository bank and transmits them to the drawee bank for accelerated processing.) The concept of an availability schedule (as previously discussed) is unique to the U.S. (at least among developed nations) and reflects this requirement for physical check movement. In contrast, other developed nations have a limited number of banks (i.e., five to 15), most of which clear one another's checks on a same-day basis.

As mergers continue among U.S. banks, the reach of institutions previously confined within a single state will become regional, as with Bank One, First Union, Fleet, and several other banks, and eventually national, as with Citigroup and Bank of America. These mergers will allow one- or two-day availability to become same- and one-day availability, reducing the time to clear a business check. (Consumers' checks will be slower to experience reduced clearing times, because many will continue to be written on smaller financial institutions that are not likely to be merged into regional or national banks.)

Comprehensive E-Commerce Products

A recent product development has been the outsourcing of payment processing, once a company determines that payments are to be received or are owed and due. Collection receipts (generically known as "comprehensive receivables") are accepted through a lockbox as straight deposits, or as electronic funds transfers (ACH and Fedwire). The bank deposits the items, merges payments and remittance data, and sends a file with this information to the company.

The outsourcing of disbursements (generically known as "comprehensive payables") involves the issue of payments the day after a bank receives a file containing instructions. The payments are entered in a diary until the appropriate release dates as indicated in the file, the disbursements are issued via any of several mechanisms, and funding of the daily clearing amount is initiated by notification to the issuer of the outstanding debit.

The cost and risk of ordering and warehousing preprinted check stock are eliminated, as the checks are laser printed on blank safety-paper stock. Remittance data are provided in the file in a preset configuration, printed by the bank and affixed to the check. Logos, signatures, and other non-standard data can be printed on the check and remittance advice. All cleared items are reconciled, and appropriate summary and detailed information are provided.

Advantages of comprehensive receivables and payables occur in the following areas:

- *Postage.* The maximum postage discount allowed by the U.S. Postal Service will be taken for disbursements, as much as 4.5 cents less than regular first-class postage (in mid-2000). This discount is often not available to issuers because the Postal Service requires a high volume of mail to each receiving zipcode.

- *Check Signing.* Current technology permits the digitizing of authorized signatures that reside within the bank's computer system. This capability relieves the requirement to physically sign checks or to protect signature plates used on check signing machines.

- *Special Messages.* Messages can be inserted on disbursement items, such as "duplicate check" or "ask us abut e-commerce partnering." These messages can change each time checks are issued, to reflect specific promotional or informational requirements.

- *Access to Electronic Payments.* Many companies are discouraged by the various requirements for electronic payments, involving protocols, VANs (value added networks), and encryption and data transmission standards. Banks that offer receipts or disbursement outsourcing can provide "turn-key" access, with the only requirement an entry in a specified field in the file showing the desired payment method.

- *Security Issues.* Accountability for the security of the payment resides with the bank so long as procedures are observed regarding file transmission and other controls. The issuing organization need have no concern regarding stolen live checks, check stock, altered checks presented for payment, or other possible security breaches.

- *Cost.* Various studies have determined that processing of paper receipts costs about $1 to $1.50; processing of paper disbursements costs about $3. The typical bank charge is about 25 to 50 cents per item for these services. (Cost estimates are exclusive of postage or other out-of-pocket charges.) A company that receives or issues 5,000 payments monthly could save tens of thousands of dollars annually, while avoiding the need for internal staff and equipment.

Process Metrics

The following metrics are useful in determining sub-optimal processes in the receipt of good funds.

• 9-1: *Percentage of Each Payment Method Used.* Various payment mechanisms may be used by your customers. Determining the frequency with which each is chosen may indicate opportunities to discourage the use of paper checks and to encourage electronics (e.g., ACH), through promotion, the offering of discounts, or appeals to convenience.

• 9-2: *Misdirected Remittances.* Poor design of billing documents inevitably causes remittances to be sent to an erroneous location, either an incorrect company address or the wrong lockbox. Misdirects may also be a deliberate attempt to extend float for the payor, as the check will likely bounce around the receiving organization for several days before it is deposited. Both situations should be monitored and aggressive remedial actions taken to reduce misdirects, including redesigning the invoice or statement and contacting your customers to request the necessary changes to their file "remit to" address. The metric that should be tracked is the number of misdirected payments.

• 9-3: *Processing (or Holdover) Time.* The time required to process mailed paper items at your offices, measured as the date received against the date deposited at the bank, may be as long as one week. Receipts are often handled by several processing stations prior to deposit. In an optimal processing cycle, all items would be deposited on the receipt date.

• 9-4: *Availability Time.* The time required to clear deposited items, or the time to attain "good" (or usable) funds, can be up to two business days (or nearly three calendar days) for U.S. commercial bank drawee points. Your banker can assist in calculating the availability you are being granted and can suggest alternative collection methods to improve this time (e.g., the use of lockboxing).

• 9-5: *Electronic Funds Recognition.* ACH, Fedwire, or other electronic funds transfers (EFTs) are clearly preferable to paper in terms of cost, float, and handling. However, the data trail that accompanies an electronic mechanism often does not provide sufficient information to identify the customer, the invoice, or the specific transactions being paid. In some cases, unknown EFTs will appear in your bank accounts, and you will have to perform a time-consuming investigation involving contacting the sender and determining the payment purpose. These problems should be monitored as a time metric to resolve unidentified receipts, including contacting payors to request better payment data and developing a database of bank accounts used by your customers to assist in your tracing efforts.

 • 9-6: *Total Collection Time.* Even though you have established efficient procedures for components of the collection cycle, the total time to collect may be slower than alternative arrangements. For example, lockboxing in one site, say Atlanta, when you have numerous customers in California and other Western states, may cost one-third of a day extra compared to the time required if you were to establish a second West Coast site. There are numerous other possible combinations of collection mechanisms that may improve your current performance. All viable options should be periodically examined and considered.

 • 9-7: *Cash Application Time.* Payments received and deposited but unapplied to receivables negatively impact your company by jeopardizing customer goodwill should inappropriate collection efforts be initiated. In addition, unapplied cash must be identified and cleared from the suspense account into which it was credited, which requires redundant clerical effort. Tracking unapplied cash allows the determination of the extent of the problem, and solutions may involve redesign of your invoices, outsourcing the process to a bank or vendor, and making appropriate refinements to your accounting system.

Gyzmo VI

Gyzmo's "net 30" credit terms were established many years earlier for the T&C business segment and carried over to P/EC. Because customers are often in a long-time relationship with the company, careful surveillance of slow payers has not been maintained, and payments are accepted at nearly any time within reason; that is, up to one month late. Customers might be late because of their own cashflow problems, because of a dispute or a return, or simply because they wish to retain the float. Smart questioned these practices but was unable to quantify the problem because of the lack of data from the receivables system.

Frustrated with the situation, Smart decided to construct a one-month sample of customer remittance history. Data from eight of the largest Gyzmo customers are shown in Exhibit 9-1. The total value of the opportunity just from these customers exceeds $1 million annually. Of course, American businesses pay late, on average some 45 days after the due date or 15 days late. However, there are some very late payers on this schedule (e.g., Bill's Cigars, Dick's Paranoia), and without an aggressive program initiated by Gyzmo to expedite payment, customers certainly would not volunteer to remit on time.

A Two-Tier Strategy

Smart spoke with the sales managers who were responsible for the slow-paying customers, but none of them was very enthusiastic about

Exhibit 9-1. Remittance practices of selected Gyzmo customers (based on invoices issued in March 2000).

P/EC customer	Invoice Dates	Payment Dates	Avg. Late Days*	Annual Sales, $ Millions	Value of 1 Day (at 9.37%)
Corleone Olive Oil	Mar. 2	Apr. 15			
	Mar. 17	Apr. 30	10	$9.50	$292,652
Clyde and Bonnie	Mar. 5	Apr. 17			
	Mar. 14	Apr. 30	11	$6.89	$233,475
Dillinger Delivery	Mar. 4	Apr. 12			
	Mar. 30	Jun. 1	18	$5.59	$309,965
Ponzi Scheme	Mar. 3	Apr. 16			
	Mar. 18	Apr. 29	9	$4.82	$133,634
Ellen's Closets	Mar. 13	Apr. 28	12	$3.40	$125,686
Bob's E.D.	Mar. 17	Apr. 26	6	$1.78	$32,900
Bill's Cigars	Mar. 25	Jun. 2	34	$1.33	$139,302
Dick's Paranoia	Mar. 28	May 31	30	$1.00	$92,416
Total				$34.31	$1,360,030

*After net 30 and assuming 3 days of mail time.

pursuing the potential opportunity. They stated that any attempt to collect earlier might jeopardize relationships, and expressed the fear that these important customers might decide to seek other sources of supply. Smart recalled his success with e-commerce marketing for the P/EC business segments and suggested that these companies might "flee" anyway once they found other vendors through the Internet that provided quality products at lower prices.

It was clear that any timely payments realized from the entire group of Gyzmo customers could develop savings that could in turn lead to lower pricing and greater profits. As a compromise, Smart proposed that the sales managers consider a two-tier pricing structure: traditional (old economy) sales and collections, that is, whenever payments are tendered; and e-commerce (new economy) sales and collections, with payments due on specified dates using electronic mechanisms. This concept was accepted by the Gyzmo senior management group.

The traditional structure would continue to sell products through established distribution channels at prices that permitted the attainment of target TVM margins. This path would continue to depend on paper-based transactions but would adapt the most aggressive procedures for improving efficiencies and cost management. The e-commerce structure would completely revise Gyzmo's marketing strategy, including terms of sale, pricing, and customer relationships. This path would attempt to increase total revenues through Internet exposure to new customers attracted to lower prices, better product descriptions and information, and faster supplier response.

Improvements in Paper Transactions

Smart first turned to Gyzmo's paper transactions. Each of the company's six business segments is responsible for its own receipts activities. With the exception of one business unit in the P/EC segment, all units instruct customers to mail their remittances to the local office address. The president of Power 'n Go established a lockbox in San Francisco, California, in 1995, relying on advice received from one of the company's bankers during a golf tournament at Pebble Beach. (Note: The deal was sealed during the wine-tasting event in Sonoma that followed.) However, many of Power 'n Go's customers continue to remit to the office address, and the company has not made any serious effort to follow up on redirecting receipts activity to the lockbox.

Mail is delivered by U.S. Postal System local route mailmen to each of the local offices between 11:00 A.M. and 2:00 P.M. daily. The mailroom personnel at each site sort the mail and deliver it to the Accounts Receivable Department, where envelopes are opened manually and contents are processed. After cash has been applied against customer accounts, the receivables clerks at each location hand deliver the checks to the Accounts Receivable manager. The Accounts Receivable manager endorses the checks, prepares a deposit slip, and takes the bundle home for the night so he or she can drop the deposit at the bank first thing in the morning, on the way to work.

The Lockbox Analysis

Smart discussed the collection systems at Gyzmo with the treasurer, I. O. Hughes. She suspects the company's collection processes are less than optimal, and, with Smart's encouragement, asked Charles S. Cheat, the assistant treasurer, to analyze the collection system used during the past year and to make recommendations for improvements. Charles talked with the company's multitude of bankers, was wined and dined, taken to baseball games, and invited to participate in 19 golf events. At the end of his "analysis," his conclusion was that "this is the best of all possible worlds." To humor I.O., he suggested that a study be commissioned of collection activities. With I.O.'s agreement, Charles hired Don I. Needajob, a financial consultant, to conduct an independent analysis of the receipts system.

After a preliminary review of Gyzmo's procedures, Don recommended that he conduct a lockbox study to determine current and optimal collection times. He explained that there were serious delays because of the midday delivery of mail and processing of checks and the process of following-day bank deposits. Gyzmo's receivables managers arranged for each business unit to forward copies of all remittance checks and original mailing envelopes received during the month of October.

Don assembled all the data in his hotel room at the Loch Ness Motel, recording the zipcode from which each customer mailed the check, the drawee bank routing transit number, the dollar amount of the check, the date the check was mailed, the date it was received and location that received it, and the date it was deposited. He sent this information to his office, where his secretary keyed it into a collection model to determine the optimal lockboxing sites.

While Don was waiting for his secretary to complete this task, he lounged around the motel swimming pool. Unfortunately, he didn't pay much attention to the sign that said:

NO LIFEGUARD ON DUTY
SWIM AT YOUR OWN RISK
Beware of the monster!

To this day, no one is sure what happened to Don. He disappeared without a trace, leaving all his belongings behind, his bill unpaid, and his report to I.O. incomplete.

The Lockbox Solution

I.O. held Charles responsible for figuring out what the printout from the Lockbox Model means. Exhibit 9-2 presents a summary of information about the current collection system. Charles must resolve the following issues:

• How many collection sites should Gyzmo have?
• Which city (or cities) should be selected?
• What is the annual savings that can be achieved by reengineering the collection system?

A review of current procedures shows that Gyzmo is currently receiving remittances at six plant sites and at a lockbox in San Fran-

Exhibit 9-2. Gyzmo current collection system performance.

Operating unit	Receipts, $000/Month	Receipts, Items/Month	Float, in $000	Collection Time, Days
T&C	$42,200	2,800	$7,396	5.43
P/EC	$20,300	3,900	$3,423	5.23
Gyzmo total	$62,500	6,700	$10,819	5.37

cisco. This results in an overall collection time of 5.37 calendar days and float totaling $10.8 million dollars. Using the current weighted average cost of capital, 9.37%, the "gross" opportunity cost of float is slightly more than $1 million a year (calculated as $10.8 million times 9.37%).

In other words, if all float were removed from Gyzmo's collection system, it could save $1 million a year. This goal is obviously not attainable by using the paper-based mail, processing, and check clearing system that predominates in the U.S. However, we can optimize the locations where mail times are minimized; we can deposit all checks on the day received; and we can reduce check clearing by using a bank lockbox arrangement.

Exhibit 9-3 summarizes information from optimal lockbox configurations for each of the Gyzmo business segments. Assuming the new lockbox costs are roughly offset by the savings of staff reductions associated with processing the remittances at each plant, the overall savings associated with conversion to six lockboxes at Atlanta is about $420,000 a year (calculated as current float of $10,819,000 minus $6,317,000, the total of float at six business units using Atlanta, at a capital cost of 9.37%).

Separate business unit lockboxes are required as each lockbox processes receivables on its own legacy system. If the entire collection system were centralized and funds were commingled into one

Exhibit 9-3. Gyzmo optimal collection system (using Atlanta as the optimal 1-site location and Atlanta/Dallas as the optimal 2-site location).

($000)	1-Site Float	2-Site Float
Cool Tool	$2,280	$2,062
Ace Fastener	$1,071	$1,039
Squeaky Wheel	$660	$641
Power 'n Go	$1,120	$1,068
Lean Green Machine	$447	$427
Puddle Muddle	$739	$689
	$6,317	$5,926

lockbox, it might be possible to save about $460,000 per year in float-related cost by using two lockboxes (e.g., Atlanta and Dallas) for all business units. (The calculation would be similar to that used for the one-lockbox system.)

The additional $40,000 in annual savings would be attractive if the costs of creating a centralized receivables system were insignificant. However, senior management may determine that a single receivables system would substantially improve collection experience and provide important customer information. Furthermore, it would have the attraction of reducing the bank expenses associated with multiple lockboxes.

Improvements in E-Commerce Transactions

Smart realized that the efficiency of a payment system based on paper transactions would always be dependent on external parties: the mails, the banks, customers, and so on. He hoped to find payment methods that would provide a greater assurance of receipts by specified dates to improve cash flow and forecasting and to eliminate uncertainty. Since his e-commerce plans had worked so well with P/EC, he decided to review the developments in electronic payments with I.O. and Charles S. Cheat. Neither of these finance "experts" was very knowledgeable, so they arranged for a briefing by a major financial institution, Second National Bank of Chicago.

The bankers told Smart that e-commerce transactions could be made through the ACH or by credit cards as specific events occurred, such as receipt of the purchase order, shipping, invoicing, or final customer acceptance. Triggers could be built into the OES to create a cash payment so long as these conditions were made clear to potential customers and the necessary banking data were captured. In fact, customers could be given the option of either payment method for smaller purchases, say up to $1,000, but be required to pay by ACH for amounts exceeding $1,000. Although the sales managers had argued for the traditional paper invoice/check cycle, they acknowledged that electronic payments would eliminate delays and ensure that timely progress payments would be received for large systems transactions.

The savings developed by timely payments allowed Gyzmo to reduce prices to e-commerce customers by $1^1/_2\%$ over traditional sales. As some of the larger clients were spending $5 to $10 million annually with the company, these savings were significant, in six figures. Furthermore, the e-commerce site reduced the customers' costs to input, verify, and review billing and payables data. The larger customers that wished to remain on the traditional plan did so, but Smart was pleased to note that several long-time relationships seemed to be strengthened by the e-commerce option.

Chapter 10

SALES, MARKETING, AND FINANCE

If a house be divided against itself, that house cannot stand.

> —*The Holy Bible: The New Testament,*
> The Gospel According to St. Mark, 3:25

Financial convention assigns non-manufacturing costs to the section of the income statement that follows the statement of manufacturing costs (the "cost of goods sold"). This chapter reviews this "house" or structure of the business enterprise, including sales and marketing costs, and financial management issues. An important financial issue, banking, is discussed in the context of the Gyzmo case.

Sales and Marketing

The principal sales and marketing issues are the process of selling; the review of the credit-worthiness of customers and prospects prior to the sale; and the pursuit of slow and non-paying customers after the sale.

Old Economy Marketing

Marketing in the old economy was used to distribute the goods resulting from mass production developed through economies of scale. Of course, products were available only in the limited styles, forms, and colors that the producer chose to manufacture, and Henry Ford's famous statement is apocryphal: "Any customer can have a car painted any color that he wants so long as it is black."[1]

1. Statement to Plant Superintendent Charles Sorensen in 1912. Cited in Allan Nevins, *Ford*, Columbia University and Ford Motor Company (1954), p. 452.

Marketing efforts often proclaimed values for products that were specious, such as that use of a certain deodorant would help one's social life. The extremely limited message content of marketing efforts forced brands and company names to try to connote value: Ivory Soap meant purity; Cadillac cars meant status and quality.

Marketing to business supposedly was more rational, but there has always been an emphasis on value creation (as we have seen in Chapters 1 and 2). The most successful use of proclaimed value in the sale to industry may well have been that of IBM. "Big Blue" led in the sale of mainframe computers beginning in the 1960s, largely on the basis of stories of success with other customers or perceived value through faster information. Once a machine was acquired, the company frequently had no idea how to use it.

New Economy Marketing

In the new economy, buyers derive product and service content from sources that are more thorough and objective, and pricing comparisons become feasible. The purchasing decision is made by increasingly knowledgeable buyers, and sellers must communicate information on product values, rather than hype. In this environment, marketing becomes integrated with the product, and continual feedback is required to bring customer expectations to manufacturing as production decisions are announced to the marketplace. The concept of manufacturing separated from sales and marketing may continue as an accounting fiction, but not in the context of managing the organization.[2]

Your sales offices, showroom, corporate facilities, and image will reside on your Website. Your prospects and customers must perceive value creation through personalized offerings, knowledge about past buying decisions, thoughtful responses to requests for product information, and accurate pricing based on order configurations and requirements. A visit to your e-commerce marketplace must be as personalized and welcoming as an old economy sales call, from greetings and a figurative handshake through the value creation of informed, real-time responses.

2. For a discussion of attitudes toward value creation for consumer goods in Internet marketing, see Douglas F. Aldrich, *Mastering the Digital Marketplace* (New York: John Wiley & Sons, 1999), Chapter 4.

The Website must be supported with supply chain management (SCM) applications to ensure that marketing promises are kept and do deliver the promised value. SCM applications do this through:

- Calculating an accurate delivery date based on available inventory and production capacity
- Selecting the optimal distribution method
- Managing lead-times and cycle times to create customer responsive operations
- Determining the profitability of a customer, an order, or a product (or product line)

Trading exchanges, supplier hubs, and other e-commerce initiatives will continue to stretch customer expectations of value. Recent e-commerce announcements, such as that concerning the formation of a trading exchange by the major auto companies,[3] indicate just how pervasively these initiatives will impact entire supply chains with 30,000 vendors expected to join the trading exchange within 18 months.

Old Economy Selling

Old economy salespeople or agents are typically motivated by the potential for commission income. Their goal is to sell product while maintaining satisfactory relationships with their customers (and their employer). Typical activities include presenting product ideas, quoting prices, and arranging for the time and condition of delivery. The sales force is usually required to contact engineering for customized systems quotes or significant variations of the standard catalog. The sales call essentially focuses on order-taking based on product available for sale or on preparing bids for systems developed based on customer requirements.

New Economy Selling

In the new economy, salespeople are integrated into the entire product planning, engineering, pricing, and marketing process. The sales

3. See Chapter 6, p. 130.

force must be knowledgeable about the capabilities of the company's manufacturing facilities. Equipped with product information and design tools (such as a laptop computer customized with the company's engineering designs), they become the primary interface between the customer and the selling company.

The salesperson's motivation continues to be compensation, more likely a "professional" salary plus bonus plan than commission. However, the goal is no longer sales—it is the entire seller-buyer relationship. Success is measured by profits to the selling organization, on-time delivery at targeted quality standards, customer satisfaction, and payment by a designated settlement date. The entire timeline cycle is managed to minimize working capital, optimize business processes, and eliminate customer complaints and rework. The goals of the sales call are transformed and now center on the development of intelligence regarding customer product needs and cooperative product design; the quoting of contract terms to meet customer requirements such as superior products, price, delivery-on-time, and payment terms; and coordination with manufacturing and engineering to fulfill contract requirements.

For sales from stock, marketing and production are joint members of the product team. They are involved in the planning of the sales campaign as the product design is being developed and are part of the sales effort so that both orders and the product can flow smoothly from sale to delivery. Sales from stock are facilitated from the vendor's designation as a preferred provider, both in traditional selling and in e-procurement. Internet access is key to product exposure to potentially wider markets. The objective is to have the seller's catalogs and product specifications (as posted on the company's Website) linked to the major purchasing hubs.

Old Economy Credit and Collections

The credit and collections function is mandatory in commercial business because companies do not collect money at the time of the sale or even at the time of delivery (except for down payments in such situations as the sale of a large system). As an old economy activity, the credit and collection process is labor-intensive, involving significant variable costs to review credit files, request analyses from credit reporting agencies, determine the amount of credit to be granted, decide whether any collateral is to be required to guarantee the credit (i.e., a bank Letter of Credit), or resolve special factors impacting the credit decision.

Efforts to collect have been automated through computer software that enables the prioritization of contacts, beginning with broken promises to pay and large overdue balances; automated telephone dialing and letter writing; automated recording of debtor responses; and callback plans. The use of these procedures allows the seller to contact more customers on an as-due basis, improving DSO by an estimated 10%.

These systems are not economical to install except for very large companies. Consequently, this work is typically outsourced to commercial collection agencies, whose systems can provide the appearance of an internal operation to customers because of the need for sensitivity in communications. Personalized scripts are used for accounts that are late by a specified number of days. Daily data transmissions between the company and the collection agency allow each party to determine the precise status of each account. Automation permits the pursuit of low-balance accounts and other overdues often deemed too unlikely to pay to be worth the effort of contacting. Costs vary by collection agency, and are often based on activity per contact rather than a percentage of monies collected.

New Economy Credit and Collections

We have previously noted the importance of nearly real-time decision-making in the new economy. This environment requires the elimination of manual processes wherever possible to speed management's ability to act and to reduce costs. In credit and collections, automation reduces costs and accelerates credit decisions through the use of scoring models; credit databases that require the purchase of incremental data instead of complete credit reports; and links to back-end issues, such as warranty claims and service requests. Many of these activities can be provided by credit and collection vendors (e.g., Dun and Bradstreet), reducing the capital committed to an in-house credit and collection function.

In the Gyzmo case we saw a typical labor-intensive credit and collection process. As e-commerce speeds and broadens market reach, the old manual procedures become obsolete. Companies that have migrated to automated decision systems for credit and collection have generally found that their results are superior to those obtained by a manual credit and collection process as measured by the rates of approval and of write-offs, and by customer satisfaction with the speed of the credit decision. This results from fewer ad hoc decisions on creditworthiness and a greater dependence on modeling and scoring. Furthermore, distribution through the Internet means selling globally, and many credit and collection functions are unable to determine who the buyer is and whether he or she is credit-worthy.

There must be an integration of all of these functions through an information network, particularly for complex systems like Gyzmo's P/EC. Current sales must be linked with payment histories and legitimate disputes or actual short payments to determine the accurate status of each customer. Disputes often require the involvement of several functions at both counterparties:

- If goods are damaged in shipment, shipping (the seller) and receiving (the buyer) must be involved.
- If the wrong goods were ordered or produced, manufacturing (the seller) and purchasing (the buyer) must participate in the resolution.
- If there was a misunderstanding regarding product functions or price, sales (the seller) and purchasing (the buyer) are needed to work out a solution.

An integrated process avoids passing the problems around for weeks until it is resolved.[4]

Financial Management

The finance function is largely transformed in the movement from the old economy to the new economy.

Old Economy Finance

Financial markets in the old economy develop complex methods of raising money to support their capital-intensive investments. The

4. There is a good discussion of these developments in David Schmidt, "Courting Automation," *Business Finance*, April 2000, pp. 49–53.

issuance of debt instruments and equity shares is a critical component of manufacturing and distribution businesses, allowing the accumulation of a large stock of funds in the corporation to acquire
plant, equipment, and other assets. Sources of debt capital include
bank loans, commercial paper and other short-term borrowings,
and corporate bonds. Equity capital is generated by retained earnings and stock sales, either in initial public offerings (IPOs) or secondary issues, or in private placements to venture capital investors.

Lenders and investors provide financing in situations where
there is a somewhat predictable income stream evaluated through a
TVM procedure (e.g., NPV or IRR; see Chapter 3). The inherent risk
in these financings is calculated by determining the present value of
capital equipment cash outflows and operations cash inflows, while
anticipating the uncertainty of unknown future events. Although
the process is burdened by risk, the success of the process in creating an industrial society in the past two centuries provides adequate
precedent to permit old economy businesses to raise capital.

New Economy Finance

In the new economy, companies will not require large amounts of
capital to finance their grand undertakings; in fact, they will partner
with other businesses for any line or staff function or process that is
not an essential element of their business. Core activities will be
managed with minimal working capital, as many of the costs of
manufacturing and distribution will be on the books of suppliers or
customers.

For example, Dell Computer does not take title to components
until production actually begins, and therefore has minimal raw materials inventory. Dell's customers' accounts are debited at the time
of shipment, usually through a credit card or an electronic funds
transfer, meaning that the company does not have to wait one to
two months for payment. Aggressive working capital management
is measured as the "cash conversion cycle" (or CCC), essentially
the days of financing to complete a sales cycle; Dell has recorded a
quarterly CCC as low as minus eight days.[5]

5. The CCC is measured as the DSO plus the days' sales inventory (the
   DSI) less the days' payables outstanding (the DPO). DSI measures the
   total time of materials and finished goods inventory; DPO measures the
   time to pay supplier invoices.

Instead of operational activities, financing will be used to fund initial experimentation and product development; acquisition of market share through pricing below cost and marketing; a cushion against early mistakes in the creation of product; and mergers of companies with attractive technology. On a "run-rate" basis, new economy companies will require much of their external financing in the start-up years. Once the business model begins to succeed, they will require capital only for acquisitions and investments in allied ventures.

The Response of Capital Markets

This change in the role of finance explains how lenders and investors perceive very uncertain cashflows, meaningless NPV and IRR calculations, and returns based on a business model previously unknown to participants. The relevant question is: How do we value a company where there are no earnings? Where a customer may view a Website 50 times and buy once (if ever)? Where the product is essentially sold at cost to attain market share?

This uncertainty is reflected in the volatility of the stock markets during the first half of 2000 and the very high valuation for Internet stocks. Naturally you would demand a 20 or 30% return in an environment where an old economy risk changes into a new economy gamble, but you would abandon situations where there is minimal hope of future returns.

The inevitable reaction by the capital markets is to reduce access to financing. Unless they work for an Internet company, finance managers are increasingly facing a chilly reception when negotiating new sources of funding. A recent survey indicated that bank lending, which until recently constituted half of all corporate borrowings, is expected to provide 37% of such funding by 2001.[6] Traditional lenders are deemphasizing credit products, citing low margins and the inability of other bank products (e.g., cash management, trade finance, custody, foreign exchange) to subsidize lending activities. Banks are becoming increasingly aware of the profitability of each corporate relationship, are using their scarce capital for mergers with other financial service companies, and, in general, are finding uses for capital other than traditional corporate lending.

6. "AFP Survey Shows Shift in Credit Resources," Association of Financial Professionals, *AFP Pulse*, February 2000, pp. 1, 7.

Alternatives for Lenders

With the ending of Glass-Steagall restrictions[7], commercial bankers are no longer prevented from pursuing other activities to generate fees. The result is that finance managers are becoming the Willy Lomans[8] of the financial world, traveling with their road shows to sell their "stories" to rating agencies, lenders, investment bankers, and journalists. Because of banks' reluctance to accept credit business, treasurers are finding that they have to significantly increase the number of potential bidders they solicit and that they must promise to re-assign non-credit business from other banks with which they have long-term relationships.

For companies forced to search for capital beyond the commercial banks, alternative sources include various non-bank lenders, including investment banks, insurance companies, mutual funds, and commercial finance companies. Some credit business that traditionally has gone to commercial banks is being placed at higher cost with non-traditional lenders. Inevitably, the allocation of capital will be based on credit-worthiness, size, and profitability as old and new economy companies compete for the finite amounts of capital that are available. However, other credit business will not be placed, and capital will not be secured.

Process Metrics

The following metrics are useful in determining sub-optimal processes in sales, marketing, and finance.

- 10-1: *Dollars of Revenue Generated to the Number of Sales Calls.* Superior marketing efforts are no longer judged on the number of customer calls but are evaluated by the success rate of the calling effort. A more responsible metric than the number of calls is the revenue-to-call ratio. Numerous reported calls with minimal revenue success is a negative indicator in determining sales perform-

7. The Glass-Steagall Act of 1933 forbade commercial banks to own, underwrite, or deal in corporate stock and corporate bonds. The law was passed in response to the 1929 stock market crash, following revelations that some banks had manipulated the prices of stocks they had underwritten.
8. The protagonist of Arthur Miller's classic tragedy *Death of a Salesman* (1949).

ance, since the assumption is that calling quality is mediocre or that prospects should have been prescreened for their potential as customers.

• 10-2: *Cost of the Sale.* Sales costs should include all of the direct expenses incurred in the marketing effort over a designated time period (e.g., one year), including the salesperson's time and travel costs, entertainment, the time and cost of materials prepared for the call or in the bidding process, and any other charge attributable to the customer. A significant increase in the average cost of a sale should generate corrective action.

• 10-3: *Total Cycle Time for Sales and Production.* The new economy focuses on integrating salespeople into the entire product planning, engineering, pricing, and marketing process. This changes the old economy metric from the length of the sales cycle to the total cycle time for sales and production.

• 10-4: *Customer Inquiry Resolution Time.* While there may not be specific invoice disputes (see Chapter 8), customers often inquire as to the status of orders, credit for returns or payments, concerns about implementation or use, or a host of other topics. The interval required to resolve these inquiries can be measured and reviewed to ascertain that buyer goodwill is maintained and that there is no deterioration in response time.

• 10-5: *Time to Complete Customer Credit Review.* The time to complete the credit review process is critical in maintaining good customer and sales force relationships. Telephoned or faxed requests for data usually are met within an acceptable turnaround time within the U.S., but turnaround can be inadequate for international credit reviews. Marginal credits may be delayed pending manager approval, which can alienate customers and prospects.

• 10-6: *Collection Cycle Time (DSO).* Days sales outstanding (DSO) or the average collection period is an established metric for the collection of accounts receivable. It is calculated as the dollar amount of receivables (as of the end of an income statement period) divided by sales per day.[9] A supplementary record of receivables

---

9. Although it would be desirable to exclude cash sales from this calculation, many companies do not report their sales components as cash and credit. Comparative ratio sources (e.g., Dun and Bradstreet, Robert Morris Associates) use total sales.

aging (usually called "the aging schedule") shows the length of outstandings in common time segments (e.g., two-week periods).

• 10-7: *Number and Success of Calls per Collection Staff.* These metrics indicate the extent of the collection effort for aged receivables. A deteriorating result may warn of inadequate credit reviews or suggest that the company is being lax or allocating insufficient resources to pursuing slow payers, indicating that outsourcing elements of the credit review and collection process may be advisable.

• 10-8: *Cost of Debt and Equity Capital.* The importance of the cost of capital was discussed in Part I.[10] The calculation of the cost of the financial structure is essential in determining the possible overuse of financial leverage and the potential risk in managing the company's debt service. This metric can be used in industry comparisons.

• 10-9: *Cost of Short-Term Funds.* We have described the developing shortage of bank financing to corporate borrowers that are less than AAA credits. This scramble for credit directly impacts the cost of short-term funds (and longer "term" loans), which may not be included or may be a small portion in the cost of debt capital calculation; see the previous metric. Obviously, the cost of short-term money is most directly impacted by Federal Reserve (or other central bank) actions in the credit markets. An important metric in managing these costs is the difference between a market rate (e.g., federal funds, LIBOR, the 91-day U.S. Treasury Bill rate) and a company's average cost of short-term funds. Should the incremental cost increase, alternative sources of financing should be sought, as previously discussed.

• 10-10: *Cost and Extent of Banking Services.* The cost of banking services has historically been partially "off- budget," as balances left on deposit have earned an interest credit (the earnings credit rate or ECR) to offset banking charges. More aggressive treasury management has reduced these balances, forcing companies to pay fees for services. However, our consulting work continues to show excessive bank costs and relationships and the use of unnecessary or inappropriate services.

10. See Chapter 1, pp. 18–20.

Gyzmo VII

Gyzmo maintains relationships with 17 banks around the country, primarily because of the decentralized nature of the organization and the autonomy granted to the business segments. These groups respond to various internal and external pressures, including purchasing, accounts payable, community relations, and, most important, the demands of the sales force. As in most companies, the salespeople drive many Gyzmo decisions, including pricing, advertising, special accommodations for important customers, and their own compensation.

Though none of the business segments negotiates individual credit facilities with its banks, each maintains its own treasury management services. Exhibit 10-1 presents a schematic diagram of the current banking system architecture. Smart realized the importance of the sales force to the past success of Gyzmo, but he also knew that much future business would be marketed on the basis of brand recognition and e-commerce. He instructed his team to investigate whether the current banking structure was appropriate given corporate needs (as opposed to the convenience of the sales force).

As a part of its research, the team determined that each business segment and the corporate home office maintain a general operating account at a local bank. This account is used for deposit of all remittances and payment of all expenses except payroll. Payroll accounts are maintained at separate banks, primarily because each of the business segments wants to deal with more than one local bank. This spread of business allows the business segment (in reality, the sales force) to have access to all of the services provided by the banks, including personal and commercial loans, mortgage financing, credit cards, and other products.

Management of the Cash Cycle

Gyzmo's finance department is located at the company's headquarters. This department has responsibility for the financial activities of all company operations, including investment of surplus cash and funding of cash shortfalls. The individual operating locations are responsible for the administration of daily receipts and disbursements, including payment initiation and bank account reconciliation, and for its own payroll processing.

Exhibit 10-1. Bank structure.

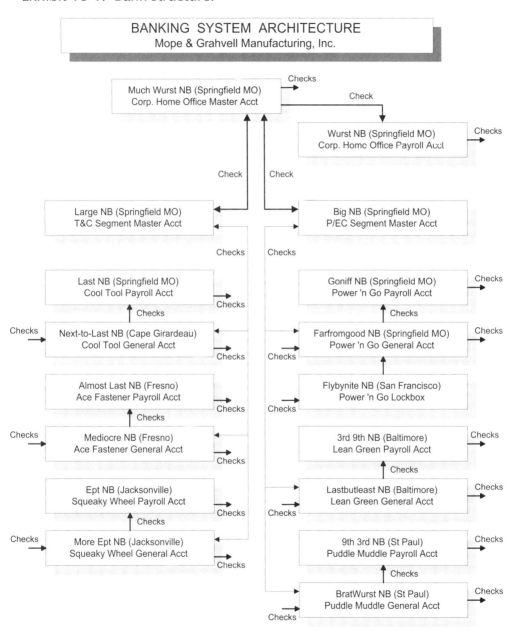

On the first business day of the month, the controller at each location reviews the prior month's ending balance at the local bank and determines whether cash is above or below the target balance level. The controllers prepare forecasts of cash requirements for the current month. They fax their month-end positions and forecasts to Charles S. Cheat by the second business day of the month.

Charles compiles a monthly cash forecast, reviews the balances in the two business segment concentration banks, and transfers cash to or from the corporate concentration bank to maintain the target balances that have been established for both segment banks.[11] The target balances have been set by the treasurer at $500,000 per bank. He does not monitor the segment bank balances because they are usually stable during the month, once all the controllers have made their deposits and withdrawals.

Concentration Bank Management

Charles gets daily balance reports on his computer from the corporate concentration bank, which has a target balance of $250,000, and estimates the cash position by 11:00 A.M. Excess cash is invested overnight in increments of $50,000. Shortfalls are covered by borrowing against a revolving line of credit at the concentration bank. The fees charged by the banks are offset by the balances left on deposit by Gyzmo.

Separate concentration accounts are maintained for T&C and P/EC so that each business segment can be operated independently. The master Gyzmo concentration account resides at a separate bank, at which Gregory Grahvell is a member of the board of directors. This "tiering" of concentration accounts results in excessive idle balances accumulating in the banks. Smart realized that the two segment concentration banks could be eliminated to free up $1 million at the two segment concentration banks ($500,000 per bank), worth nearly $100,000 a year, based on the company's cost of capital of 9.37%.

11. A *concentration account* holds all incoming or outgoing movements of funds from other bank accounts to assist in mobilizing cash to fund disbursements or for investment. Generally, this account is funded by deposits of incoming wire transfers, collection account transfers, and branch deposit concentration. The account provides funds by outgoing wire and ACH transfers.

Other Cash Issues

Smart also concluded that plant controller month-end reporting of local balances is inadequate for maintaining control over cash balances. Excess or deficit cash positions should be handled by electronic funds transfers rather than paper checks. Balance management would become much more controllable if collections were moved to lockboxes at a single site and disbursements paid through a single bank. More timely and improved cash forecasting processes would permit more aggressive short-term investment management, yielding better returns than those available through overnight investments late in the day. This change would minimize the need to borrow from the line of credit.

Multiple local accounts for payroll and payables activities and tiered concentration accounts creates too many bank accounts, too many funding activities, and too expensive a banking system. The costs of the current system are $40,000 a month (Exhibit 10-2), nearly $500,000 a year! According to a recently published benchmarking analysis of banking costs, other companies of Gyzmo's size were spending about $200,000 a year.

Before Smart's arrival, Gyzmo had been experiencing serious cash shortages and had to draw down perilously close to the limit against their credit line. Since his involvement with every aspect of the timeline, the company's financial position had significantly improved. He could report to Grahvell and Mope that their strategy to maximize shareholder value had so far been successfully executed. Smart realized that senior management would have to remain alert against the return of the "silo" mentality,[12] which was responsible for many of the problems he and his team had encountered.

12. See Chapter 1, pp. 26–28.

Exhibit 10-2. Bank fees and balances.

Business Unit, Segment	Purpose	Average Balance ($000)	Bank*	Monthly Fees
Cool Tool, T&C	Payroll	$150	Last NB	$2,000
Cool Tool, T&C	Payables; local collections	$500	Next-to-Last NB	$3,000
Ace Fastener, T&C	Payroll	$150	Almost Last NB	$1,500
Ace Fastener, T&C	Payables; local collections	$200	Mediocre NB	$3,000
Squeaky Wheel, T&C	Payroll	$150	Ept NB	$1,500
Squeaky Wheel, T&C	Payables; local collections	$200	More Ept NB	$1,000
Power 'n Go, P/EC	Payroll	$150	5th Bourbon NB	$1,000
Power 'n Go, P/EC	Payables; local collections	$200	Far-from-good NB	$1,000
Power 'n Go, P/EC	Lockbox collections	$500	Flybynite NB	$4,000
Lean Green, P/EC	Payroll	$150	3rd 9th NB	$1,500
Lean Green, P/EC	Payables; local collections	$200	Last-but-least NB	$2,000
Puddle Muddle, P/EC	Payroll	$100	9th 3rd NB	$1,500
Puddle Muddle, P/EC	Payables; local collections	$200	BratWurst NB	$2,500
Corp. Home Office	Central payroll	$100	Wurst NB	$1,000
Corp. Home Office	Master Acct; payables	$250	Much Wurst NB	$3,500
T&C Segment	Master Account	$500	Large NB	$5,000
P/EC Segment	Master Account	$500	Big NB	$5,000
Total		$4,200		$40,000

*NB = National Bank.

Chapter 11

SERVICE INDUSTRY COST ELEMENTS

Certainly there are lots of things in life that money won't buy, but it's very funny—
have you ever tried to buy them without money?

—Ogden Nash (1902–1971),
Happy Days, the Terrible People

Our focus in this book has primarily been on manufacturing industries because they are defined by a regular cycle of materials, work-in-process, invoicing, and the receipt of funds. Services industries do not experience a consistent set of sequential activities, and it is more difficult to generalize about the functioning of these companies. Each service industry has particular functions, requirements, nomenclature, and payment terms for the settlement of transactions.

The Rise of Services Industries

The old economy was based on the mass production and distribution of goods. The vast structures needed to develop competitive economies of scale required enormous manufacturing output, accompanied by a distribution system that essentially had to be created to move product. Recall that prior to the Industrial Age, shopkeepers and artisans produced and sold their very limited supply of goods without any form of promotion, without the need to consider pricing strategies, and with little product innovation.

The retail "revolution" led by Sears Roebuck included catalog and mail order sales, a sophisticated inventory and order-filling system, rapid delivery through the U.S. Postal Service, and, later, a network of retail stores. Retail discounting was reinvented by Wal-Mart, with high quality, low prices, and customer-friendly touches such as "store greeters." Consumer demand was stimulated by advertising, initially through print and later by broadcast and telecast media.

Old Economy Services

Services industries followed in support of mass production and distribution, offering finance, maintenance, and repair activities. Although such support services were originally an afterthought, the growing wealth of the Western economies and the outsourcing of business functions fostered substantial service industry expenditures. Retail and corporate customers became unable or unwilling to provide these activities for themselves. For example, autos were originally maintained by their owners; today, the need to access sophisticated equipment and the requirement in warranties for service by qualified mechanics has created a $50 billion business.[1]

The old economy built structures and acquired equipment to provide these services, such as printing presses for publishing; film studios and processing facilities in the entertainment sector; hospitals in healthcare delivery; and bank branches in retail banking. While expertise is clearly necessary to provide the service, access to the physical asset (and the capital to acquire those assets) is critical.

New Economy Services

New economy services industries are primarily information oriented, focusing on the creation of the value-added knowledge content provided to customers. There is no core requirement to invest in structure or equipment, and customers do not look to a physical presence for confidence in their choice of vendor. The entire financial services sector (i.e., banks, securities dealers, finance companies, insurers) can be cited as evidence of this shift in focus. We look to the securities industry to execute trades, raise capital, purchase foreign exchange, and provide investment advice, all information-driven activities. We do not care where their workers are located, how large or impressive their buildings are, or the level of sophistication of their computer hardware.

Information rather than structure leads to the potential for significant changes in services industry business processes. For example, automobile dealers are in business to provide services to businesses and consumers, from vehicle distribution and mainte-

---

1. Extrapolated from data in U.S. Bureau of the Census, *1992 Enterprise Statistics*.

nance to financing, rental, and resale. There are no inherent economies in this form of organization, and, in fact, new car sales have long been subsidized by other dealer activities. Each of these services could be conducted by more efficient providers; e.g., car inventory scale economies are optimized in regional superdealerships, and financing can be arranged by Internet lenders.[2]

Service Industry Cycles

As we noted in Chapter 1, the old economy "value added" is expertise, relationship, and market position. These competitive advantages will be severely challenged in the new economy through Internet connectivity, and customers will gravitate toward companies with the advantages of low cost, convenience, and a reputation for quality and speed. This trend will force old economy services companies to develop efficient operations, improve service, and become price competitive, which can be accomplished only by the analysis of the timing within the specific cycles of each service business. Three examples are presented in the next sections.[3]

Insurance: The Plan

Group health insurance is frequently provided as an administrative service (known as ASO or alternate funded business). Traditional coverage (e.g., life insurance) is usually sold as a fully insured product, with the insurer entirely responsible for any losses incurred by the insured. In ASO, the insurance company is engaged by the corporate client to provide the service of managing insurance coverage to its employees, paying providers (e.g., hospitals, physicians) or employees as claims are settled. However, any funds paid out by the insurer are reimbursed by the corporation, with the claim service priced as an administrative fee without the insured segment.

As we discussed in Chapters 3 through 5, the calculation of gross margin, return-on-sales, and return-on-equity is critical in de-

2. See Bernard Wysocki, Jr., "The Big Bang," special "Amazing Future" issue of *The Wall Street Journal*, January 1, 2000, p. R34.
3. The insurance and commercial finance company examples were first presented in a different format in James S. Sagner, *Cashflow Reengineering* (New York: AMACOM, 1997), pp. 95–99.

termining TVM returns. Consider an insurance company that has a target to hold of two days of average claim payments while awaiting the replenishment of advances made by the insurer on settled claims. This results in a target gross margin percentage of 0.65%, which, while appearing to be low, is fairly significant compensation for the limited role performed by the insurer, especially when applied against a $500 million annual cashflow. With invested capital of $30 million for that segment of the business, the resulting target return-on-equity is 10.8%.

Insurance: The Outcome

A financial analysis similar to that conducted for Gyzmo showed that incorrect assumptions had been made regarding the financial obligations assumed by the insurer for this business. In addition, there was inadequate surveillance of the timing of the actions by the insurer and the responses of the client. Furthermore, the insurer did not fully understand the extent of bank balances advanced and bank fees absorbed prior to reimbursement by the corporate client. The target gross margin of 0.65% became an actual loss of 0.50%, even before sales and other general and administrative expenses were paid.

   Exhibit 11-1.a through 11-1.d timeline elements make varying contributions to the length of the cycle, 3.7 days versus the target of 2.0 days. Client funds advanced (11-1.a) acts positively, in that monies have been advanced in expectation of claim payments made to insureds or providers. Insurer bank fees paid (11-1.b) are the charges for maintaining bank accounts on behalf of client organizations from which claims are paid. Bank charges primarily are for checks paid and for wire transfers received (or other funding mechanisms).

   Insurer bank balances advanced (11-1.c) represent the cost of monies advanced by the insurer to cover claim checks issued. If these payments had not been made, insured and provider checks would not have been honored by the issuing bank. In all cases, the advance is repaid by the client company, but the insurer is out the funds for an average of 2.4 days. Insurer ASO costs (11-1.d) are the various administrative cost categories incurred in operating this business, including personnel, systems, and other expenses.

   Outcomes for the insurer might improve if it were to take the

Exhibit 11-1. Services company work-days and gross margin impact (insurance company).

Detail of Income Statement		Work-Days	GM% Impact
Target gross margin		2.0	0.65
Less			
Client funds advanced	(11-1.a)	−0.7	−0.25
Insurer bank fees paid	(11-1.b)	0.9	0.30
Insurer bank Balances advanced	(11-1.c)	2.4	0.80
Insurer ASO costs	(11-1.d)	1.1	0.30
Total work-days		3.7	
Equals			
Realized gross margin			−0.5

following steps: require corporations to provide reimbursement by wire transfer on the day that claims are paid or advance two to three days of funds prior to payment (based on data from the checks issued file); pay claims off the company's bank account to eliminate the use of insurer funds; or base reimbursements on issued (rather than paid) disbursements, allowing one or more days of additional funding to the insurer.

Expense avoidance and/or additional revenue are required to develop a profitable business environment, involving the coordinated efforts of marketing, systems, claims, and finance. In the absence of these initiatives, the result may be price increases or abandonment of the market. Many insurance companies that wrote health coverage have in fact ceased selling such insurance because it is insufficiently profitable.

The Securities Industry: The Plan

The securities (or broker-dealer) industry operates under various regulations in terms of both the timely clearing and settlement of trades and the segregation and protection of customer funds. As with our insurance example, there are various elements in the management of brokerage activities that assume the optimal use of funds. However, any slippage can cause the deterioration of margins, a particular concern since the funding requirements for large broker-dealers can be in the tens of billions of dollars.

One firm's funding desk transacted $5 billion in overnight bank borrowing and an equivalent amount in intercage (i.e., intrafirm) transfers and such other activities as commercial paper and master trust notes. (A "cage" is a secure facility that handles cash and securities for specific groups of products.) Individual cages estimate their funding needs on the basis of the trading activities expected to settle that day, adjusted by an anticipated level of "fails" and "DK" trades. ("Fails" are trades that do not settle because of the failure to present cash or securities in good form on settlement day; "DKs" or "don't knows" are trades for which critical data are missing.)

A cage typically prepares a preliminary funding estimate in the morning hours and refines it throughout the day as additional information becomes available. A final funding number is reported any time after midafternoon. The funding desk arranges for funds throughout the day, but most typically after the afternoon report. Although money rates fluctuate due to global economic conditions and markets, there is a lower cost in the morning by 20 to 40 basis points (bp). (A "basis point" is 1/100th of a percentage point.) This situation exists because markets are much more liquid early in the day, with many more participants.

The Securities Industry: The Outcome

The total annual impact on the gross margin for this firm was 0.4%, or nearly $6.5 million. Funding activities are not directly related to revenues from securities transactions and are essentially costs of doing business. As a result, the gross margin is not included in Exhibit 11-2. Although the work-day equivalent for the inefficiencies noted is only about one hour, the huge daily funding requirement results in this large improvement opportunity for the firm.

The assumed funding cost for the major portion of securities firms is the federal funds rate plus 20 to 25 bp, or 6.20 to 6.25% (at midyear 2000). Late funding (11-2.a) affects about one-half of the amount borrowed (about $3.5 billion daily), resulting in higher costs of $4 million a year. In addition, there are costs related to same-day

Exhibit 11-2. Services company work-days and gross margin impact (securities industry funding desk).

Detail of Income Statement		*Work-Days*	*GM% Impact*
Incremental funding cost	(11-2.a)	0.1250	.0025
Same-day borrowing/investing	(11-2.b)	0.0050	.0010
Redundant cage personnel cost	(11-2.c)	0.0025	.0005
Total work-days			
Total incremental costs		0.1325	.0040

borrowing and investing (11-2.b), due to improved forecasting and the consolidation of all funding in a single desk. The amount of this unnecessary funding was approximately $500 million per occasion, and there was one occurrence for every 10 trading days. Additional costs were incurred to maintain separate funding personnel and facilities in the various cages (11-2.c).

Various recommendations were implemented to develop these savings. These included earlier cage reporting of transaction calculations to the funding desk; the use of forecasting for trade settlements based on known trading activity and on historical data for fails and DKs; and the consolidation of funding in a single desk. In addition, this process assisted in reducing the natural "silo" barriers that typify securities firms, encouraging cross-selling and the development of new investment products.

Commercial Finance: The Plan

In the commercial finance industry, various types of lending are made to dealers that sell vehicles and large equipment. The automobile industry refers to these arrangements as "floor planning." Due to business practice, manufacturers expect payment on delivery to their dealers, forcing vehicles to be financed until sold.

Cost elements include the following:

• *Method of Payment: "Paid-as-Sold" or "Scheduled Liquidation."* Paid-as-sold liquidates loans as inventory is sold; scheduled liquidation repays loans on the basis of specific calendar timing regardless of sales success. Paid-as-sold is preferred by clients, since repayments are not made until inventory is liquidated, normally as retail sales. Scheduled liquidation is preferred by commercial finance companies, since cashflows are "assured" on specific dates, assuming clients make the payments as specified by contract.

• *Interest Charges.* A major impact on the realized gross margin percentage, interest charges are set by formula but may be negotiated with the client in order to win or retain business.

• *Late Fees.* Late fees relate to the failure to make timely scheduled liquidation payments on the basis of contractural terms. Paid-as-sold payments are also subject to late fees if, on audit, it is determined that inventory has been sold but timely payment has not been made.

• *Rebates of Floor Planning Charges.* Manufacturer and distributors often rebate interest charges incurred by dealers to promote sales. These are shown as a negative calculation.

Commercial Finance: The Outcome

The profitability of specific deals, and of categories of deals by manufacturer, by product, by geographic region, and by dealer, will vary from the target gross margin, and returns are often inadequate. In this example, the target gross margin of 5% was actually 2%, significantly below the business goal of the commercial finance company.

Exhibit 11-3.a through 11-3.d timeline elements contribute to the length of the cycle, 18.0 days versus a target of 10.8 days. Areas of potential improvement include: more vigorous auditing of scheduled liquidation clients to ascertain that payments are made as inventory is liquidated (11-3.a); greater control over negotiation of interest charges and other changes by sales (11-3.b); and collection of appropriate late fees (11-3.c). In general, there should be a required threshold profitability by deal to justify each financing agreement.

Work Cycle Commonality

There is no commonality linking the insurance, securities industry, and commercial finance cases, nor is there any in other service industries we have analyzed as consultants. Furthermore, situations

Exhibit 11-3. Services company work-days and gross margin impact (commercial finance).

Detail of Income Statement		Work-Days	GM% Impact
Target gross margin		10.8	5.00
Less			
Method of payment	(11-3.a)	4.5	0.75
Interest charges	(11-3.b)	9.0	1.50
Late fees	(11-3.c)	6.0	1.00
Rebates of floor planning charges	(11.3.d)	−1.5	−0.25
Total work-days		18.0	
Equals			
Realized gross margin			2.00

of regulation or practice proscribe certain elements of the work-task cycle. For example, healthcare delivery demands specific practices to support government or insurance company reimbursement, and the clearing and settlement of securities trades follows rules established by the Securities and Exchange Commission, the stock exchanges, and other regulatory bodies.

Each component within the cost structure of a service industry will vary depending on its specific requirements and "factors of production." In developing an analysis for these industries, it is essential to determine which procedures are mandated, which are based on established practice or competitive pressure, and which may be revised depending on the outcome of a detailed analysis.

As common cycles are not typically found in services industries, it is difficult to generalize about the functioning of these companies. As a result, the identification of process metrics is quite challenging, unlike the situation for manufacturing industries. A further problem is the tendency of many service industry companies to expend rather than capitalize their costs, resulting in organizational costing but not accurate output costing.[4] This is the common

4. This concern was documented through the survey of 50 companies in the services sector. See Otto B. Martinson, *Cost Accounting in the Service Industry* (Montvale, N.J.: Institute of Management Accountants, 1994), pp. 47–48, 81.

practice, despite the fact that work-in-process may well exist at the end of an accounting period. Examples include the following:

- *Accounting.* An audit may be in progress.
- *Engineering.* Facility design or the preparation of blueprints may be only partially drafted.
- *Banking.* Loan documents may be in the process of finalization and circulation for comment.
- *Insurance.* The underwriting and pricing of life and health insurance for a large company may be in review and negotiation.

Most service companies treat such expenses as period costs. As a result, it is difficult to properly assign costs to the revenue received upon completion of the service and to use those data to construct useful process metrics.

Process Metrics

The following metrics are useful in determining sub-optimal processes in the services industries.

- 11-1: *Billable Days versus Non-Billable Days for Professional Service Businesses.* This metric determines the time and potential waste in sales, meetings, and other non–client-related activities (other than vacation or sick time) in professional services, including law, accounting, consulting, medical and dental practices, and engineering firms.
- 11-2: *Budgeted Days versus Actual Days to Complete Projects and Engagements.* All service businesses should track the ratio of actual hours spent as compared to budgeted hours to determine the accuracy of the estimating process, the possible cause of low profitability or losses, and the opportunity for remedial actions.
- 11-3: *Customer Profitability.* As described in the insurance industry situation, profitability objectives often are subverted by subtle business influences, including delays throughout the work cycle from service delivery through invoicing and the receipt of funds. Because of the numerous functions involved in the management of each work cycle element, the cumulative impact of these delays may

not be fully understood by management. It is therefore necessary to compare actual and target profits by individual customer to spot developing problems.

• 11-4: *Segment Profitability.* This metric measures profitability by segment (or region or other relevant grouping) and is intended to include all relevant marketing and operational activities provided. Service companies developing these data typically determine that certain groups of customers (by size, industry, or geographic location) do not provide adequate "run-rate" revenues to cover the all-in costs of doing business.

• 11-5: *Service Profitability.* Companies often provide "families" of services, some of which are priced to entice the use of the full range of offerings or to meet market competition. For example, in banking, certain corporate services earn substantial profits (e.g., wholesale lockbox, custody, shareholder services), while others are marginal (e.g., ACH, controlled disbursement). Determining the profitability of each service allows management to make thoughtful decisions, such as whether to adjust the price.

• 11-6: *Length of Billing and Expense Reimbursement Cycle.* If professional services are billed to clients, the duration of the cycle to collect data regarding hours worked and expenses incurred is a critical determinant of total collection time. Various automated systems are now available to expedite this process.

• 11-7: *Number of Items Serviced in a Work-Day.* This metric calculates throughput and is useful in longitudinal studies of improvement or deterioration in efficiency; the need to reduce or increase labor, equipment, or supervision, and the potential for work-cycle delays.

• 11-8: *Number of Customer Service Requests and Resolution.* Customers may request services that are normally provided in the course of business, such as repairs, credit for returns or resolution of disputes, or duplicate invoice copies. Requests may also be made for services not typically rendered, such as assistance with financing, installation, or customization. It is important to track these events to ensure that appropriate responses are provided and that opportunities for additional business are not overlooked.

Gyzmo VIII

The cost of the large systems of P/EC and Squeaky Wheel often impeded sales to customers who were otherwise convinced of their business usefulness. Some of the assembled and installed systems were priced in excess of $500,000, which often made budget approval difficult, particularly as customer costs of capital were rising (as were Gyzmo's capital costs). The company's sales agents could handle just about any objection except cost, and they frequently tried to assist customers with financing through their own bank contacts or other credit relationships.

Smart's team became aware of this situation during sales visits. The goal of these trips had been to increase awareness of customer perceptions of Gyzmo. However, it quickly became apparent that the financing objection was a principal sales barrier. Customers often started conversations with questions about borrowing arrangements, leasing and tax considerations, and other issues not directly related to system functionality. As the sales agents were trained in the engineering and product features of these large systems, they were often unable to assist customers without support from the corporate office. And, given the level of knowledge of commercial finance of the corporate Treasurer, I. O. Hughes, that wasn't much help!

Should Gyzmo Finance Its Sales?

Smart decided to analyze the possibility of establishing a sales financing function at Gyzmo specifically for large systems purchases, those for which the price was $250,000 or more. He envisioned a modest function involving financial and credit specialists for deal analysis and legal counsel for contract and note drafting. Pricing would be the same as for "cash" transactions, and interest charges and other fees would be based on the costs related to the financing function plus a small profit for the service.

Credit would initially be provided by a financial institution once the decision was made regarding a customer's credit-worthiness. By using a single funding source, it was expected that the cost of funds would be minimized, resulting in attractive interest costs to Gyzmo's customers. Smart knew that some companies established their own credit companies (e.g., GMAC) and issued their own debt instruments, but he did not believe that Gyzmo would grow to the size necessary to justify such a function for several years (if ever).

Sales Financing Costs

After reviewing equivalent competitive operations, the following cost elements were identified.

• *Interest Charges.* Interest charges for the amount financed could be set by formula tied to Gyzmo's cost of capital but could also be negotiated with the customer in order to win or retain business.

• *Late Fees.* Late fees relate to the customer's failure to make timely payments based on scheduled terms. (Smart was warned that late fees had to be set high enough to dissuade late payers, who might otherwise "ride" on Gyzmo's credit.)

• *Credit Review/Collateral.* Financed sales require credit reviews of customers who are acquiring Gyzmo systems and, in certain instances, access to appropriate collateral to ensure timely payment.

• *Legal Actions.* Payment or performance disputes may result in actions for remedies by either Gyzmo or their customers, resulting in various legal costs.

• *Repossession Costs.* Following payment default, it may be necessary for Gyzmo to repossess equipment and systems technology. The value of such assets may be seriously compromised by such action, and these costs must be included in the analysis.

Sales Financing Potential Revenue

The target gross margin for large Gyzmo systems was established in Chapter 5 as 15%. Utilizing customary fees for providing sales financing activities, Smart's team estimated appropriate expenses; see Exhibit 11-4. With a reasonable profit margin added to the usual financing expenses, Smart realized that the potential fee revenue from sales financing could be more than 50% of the margin from the traditional manufacturing and sales of large systems.

Since current P/EC and Squeaky Wheel gross margins exceeded $40 million, the potential benefit to Gyzmo of creating a financing operation would be substantial. If one-third of large system customers used Gyzmo's sales financing, fees would exceed $8 million. Basing calculations on that level of activity, the net profit could exceed $1 million! These amounts would likely significantly in-

Exhibit 11-4. Estimated Gyzmo large systems sales financing costs.

Detail of Income Statement	GM% Impact
Target gross margin	15.00%
Sales Financing Costs	
Interest charges	1.50%
Late fees	2.50%
Credit review/collateral	0.50%
Legal actions	2.00%
Repossession	1.00%
Total	7.50%

crease as total large system revenues rose in the future, with the neutralizing of a major sales "objection" (cost).

Outsourcing Considerations

Smart also knew that less than vigorous administration of the program could result in substantial losses to Gyzmo and that sales financing is really a different business from the manufacturing and distributing of tools and complex systems. He was concerned that any mistakes made in this new business could seriously impact Gyzmo's liquidity. His team was instructed to consider other alternatives, including the outsourcing of sales financing activities.

Gyzmo's credit line bank, Wurst National Bank, declined involvement in this venture, claiming a lack of capability. Smart began to realize that he might need to consider regional or national banking institutions for financing services. Various commercial finance companies and financial institutions were contacted to discuss their financing products, and six were asked to bid on packages of outsourcing services to Gyzmo. From their responses, Smart began to focus on equipment leasing.

Leasing

In a leasing arrangement, the equipment could be purchased for the customer, who would pay rent for a predetermined useful life. (A variation is the sale-leaseback, where Gyzmo's customers invoice the commercial finance company for the equipment for as much as 100% of the current value upon credit and transaction approval.) Leasing would offer several financial advantages to the customer compared to paying cash or getting a loan, including comprehensive financing, no down payment, 100% tax deductions, cash requirements, no weakening of the customer's debt ratio, minimal equipment obsolescence, and maximum hedge against inflation.

Such arrangements cost slightly more than a standard lease, but less than other methods such as bank loans, especially considering the short completion time (less than 10 days) and simple documentation involved. Restrictions on customer budget limitations can be circumvented, and working capital can be released for other uses. These benefits result primarily because the commercial finance company (the lessor) and not Gyzmo's customer (the lessee) owns the equipment.

Smart concluded that the experience required to manage a sales financing activity could not be easily developed in-house and that the risk of loss was substantial unless a high level of expertise was involved. He arranged for a leading commercial finance company to handle all of the financing requirements of Gyzmo's large system customers. One of the most important benefits was the provision of Internet access, allowing these customers to hyperlink to their Website once the e-commerce sales function had started. In this way, customers in one Internet session could specify systems requirements; understand contractual, delivery, and installation issues; and arrange for financing.

AFTERWORD TO PART II

Look to the essence of a thing, whether it be a point of doctrine, of practice, or of interpretation.

—Marcus Aurelius (121–180), *Meditations*

To summarize our Part II discussion, 50 process metrics are used to evaluate the major transaction cycle elements to help determine sub-optimal processes resulting in inefficient work-day cycles. Chapters 6 through 9 addressed manufacturing cycles; Chapter 10 reviewed marketing and administrative cycles, and Chapter 11 discussed service industry cycles.

Whenever possible (in about one-half of the measures), time quantification is used as the process metric. The determination of work cycle days is a basic foundation of financial metrics, addressed in Part I, and allows the calculation of the dollar equivalent in float cost (as evaluated at the company's cost of capital). When time is not the appropriate metric, such quantities as percentages, ratios, and item counts are used.

These metrics should be charted over time by the company to determine deteriorating patterns in performance. It is not advised that comparisons between companies be performed because of the variations inherent in all companies. However, some of these metrics are reported as standard ratios and can be compared to industry norms compiled by Dun and Bradstreet, Robert Morris Associates, or other services.

Process metrics should not be confused with benchmarking or "best practices," which compare a company's performance, output, or efficiency to that of a peer group or set of competitors. Companies that focus on the number of transactions completed or the equivalent cost, rather than on the content of those transactions, are forcing employees to focus on quantity rather than quality. We have observed several companies where the process has turned into a team competition and the winning group receives recognition at the end of the month. In those situations, the result is speed, but at the sacrifice of the work product.

Benchmarking and best practices are forms of microanalysis, which involves the examination of a very specific element that exists within the larger context of the cashflow timeline, first discussed in Chapter 1. The essence of the timeline concept is an entire process, not a single step or action within that process. If you focus on specific elements rather than the process, you may find that not all alternative approaches are identified, that timeline element interactions are not considered, and that not all elements within each alternative are examined.

The process metrics are listed in the table that follows, in approximate timeline chronology. For an explanation of each metric, see the appropriate chapter.

Chapter reference/ sequence number	Description of metric	Quantification
Chapter 6: Materials Purchases		
6-1, 1	Materials utilization	Days; % of space utilized
6-2, 2	Vendor errors	% of materials problems; no. of items in error
6-3, 3	Materials movement time	Days
6-4, 4	Commodity analysis	Price ratio; % hedged purchased
6-5, 5	Expedited purchasing	Days
6-6, 6	Completion of purchase order/receiver file	% of complete P.O. files
6-7, 7	Local purchasing	% of use of purchasing card (of total purchasing)
6-8, 8	Issuance of accounts payable remittances	Days
6-9, 9	Cash discounts taken	% of discounts taken of total offered
Chapter 7: Work-In-Process		
7-1, 10	Direct labor expended	Days; % of overtime and idle time

Chapter reference/ sequence number	*Description of metric*	*Quantification*
7-2, 11	Payroll mechanisms	% of each mechanism used
7-3, 12	Damage in movement	% of damage; no. of re-works
7-4, 13	Assembly line or machinery downtime	% of downtime
7-5, 14	Inspection failures requiring remedial action	No. of failures
7-6, 15	Target vs. actual WIP	Days
7-7, 16	Finished goods inventory	Days
7-8, 17	Finished goods shipped by premium carrier	% of shipments by premium carrier
7-9, 18	Timely receipt of progress payments	Days

Chapter 8: Invoice Preparation

8-1, 19	Pre-invoice preparation time	Days
8-2, 20	System downtime causing invoicing delays	Days
8-3, 21	Invoicing after optimal date	Days
8-4, 22	Mail delay	Days
8-5, 23	Disputed invoices resolution time	Days
8-6, 24	Customer service contacts regarding invoice disputes	No. of contacts

Chapter 9: Receipt of Good Funds

9-1, 25	Timing of payment receipt vs. due date	Days
9-2, 26	Mis-directed remittances	No. of mis-directs

Chapter reference/ sequence number	*Description of metric*	*Quantification*
9-3, 27	Payment methods used	% of each
9-4, 28	Processing (holdover) time	Days
9-5, 29	Availability time	Days
9-6, 30	Electronic funds recognition	Days
9-7, 31	Total collection time	Days
9-8, 32	Cash application time	Days

Chapter 10: Sales, Marketing, and Finance

10-1, 33	Dollars of revenue generated to the number of sales calls	Ratio
10-2, 34	Cost of the sale	$ of cost
10-3, 35	Total sales and production cycle time	Days
10-4, 36	Customer inquiry resolution time	Days
10-5, 37	Time for customer credit review	Days
10-6, 38	Collection cycle time (DSO)	Days
10-7, 39	Success of calls per credit/ collection staff	No. of (successful) calls
10-8, 40	Cost of debt and equity capital	cost %
10-9, 41	Cost of short-term funds	Incremental cost %
10-10, 42	Cost and extent of banking services	$ of fees and balances equivalent; array of services

Chapter 11: Service Industry Cost Elements

11-1, 43	Billable vs. unbillable days for professional service businesses	% of billable days

Chapter reference/ sequence number	Description of metric	Quantification
11-2, 44	Budgeted vs. actual days to complete projects/ engagements	Ratio of budgeted to actual days
11-3, 45	Customer profitability	ROS %
11-4, 46	Segment profitability	ROS %
11-5, 47	Service profitability	ROS %
11-6, 48	Length of billing and expense reimbursement cycle	Days
11-7, 49	Items serviced in a work-day	No. of items
11-8, 50	Customer service requests and resolution	No. of requests

Part III

Winners and Losers

I wonder what goes on in the business world?

E-commerce re-writes all of the rules of business, forcing real-time decision-making and consideration of financial and process metrics. Chapter 12 analyzes the future of the changing business environment and suggests who will be the winners and the losers.

THE CHALLENGE OF THE NEW ECONOMY

Since I do not foresee atomic energy is to be a great boon for a long time, I have to say that for the present it is a menace.

—Albert Einstein (1879–1955),
"Einstein on the Atomic Bomb," *Atlantic Monthly*

You are not likely to encounter very many I. M. Smarts (or Albert Einsteins) in the real world of business. As financial consultants to global Fortune 500 companies, governments, and not-for-profits, we typically work with organizations unwilling to move away from what has been successful in the past and more-or-less routine to manage. We are not implying negligence. Rather, there is simply an apathy and opposition to change that ultimately can seriously impact or even destroy a company.

Realities of the New Economy

Many twenty-first-century managers continue to manifest traits acquired from years of repeated activities. Some of the more common behaviors we've seen include:

- Continuing old business relationships despite access to global sources of supply and potential customers
- Retaining inefficient business practices despite indications that better methods may be available
- Purchasing and installing technology without appropriate consideration for the needs of the organization
- Having financial systems that provide data that are useless for decision-making
- Instituting changes fostered by senior executives who have insufficient knowledge about the activities of their organizations or how to implement new strategies

The mad rush to new economy business ignores the complexities of the modern corporation. While the importance of e-commerce is undeniable, the real benefits will be to those organizations that carefully analyze their costs, markets, products, channels of distribution, access to capital, and sources of supply. Once the company has a thorough understanding of these dynamics through such systems as enterprise resource planning (ERP) (see the appendix to this chapter), it can utilize e-commerce. Applying e-commerce to a sub-optimal structure can only exacerbate current inadequacies and may lead to adverse consequences.

The developments described throughout the Gyzmo case are driven by revisions to the capital structure and transaction finance (Chapters 4 and 5), timeline efficiencies (Chapters 5 through 11), and e-commerce initiatives (Chapters 5, 9, and 10). There is no one magic bullet here. Rather, various actions are taken to make Gyzmo efficient, with a total annual benefit of $23 million; see Exhibit 12-1. That represents 43% of the earnings reported for the year prior to Mr. Smart's arrival!

Structure of the Balance Sheet

We reviewed the structure of Gyzmo's balance sheet and its cost of capital as measured against a peer group of similar companies. We found that the aggressive use of debt financing was causing a high cost of capital that could be rectified only by increasing the proportion of equity: retained earnings or new common stock.

Transaction Finance

The work-day requirements for each element of the timeline were determined for manufacturing, sales activities, and administration expenses. Delays causing long cycle time were identified and measured according to transaction finance procedures. Specific actions were initiated to manage these delays, including the use of the mechanisms of e-commerce and electronic funds transfer.

Purchasing, Payables, and Payroll

Various recommendation were made to optimize the handling of purchasing, accounts payable, and payroll. These included developing economic order quantity decision rules, requiring competitive

Exhibit 12-1. Summary of Gyzmo actions.

Chapter	Topic	Recommendation	Annual benefit
4	Balance sheet structure	Restructure balance sheet	$5.85 MM*
4	Transaction finance analysis I	Reduce manufacturing timeline work-days	$9.6 MM ledger**
5	Transaction finance analysis II	Reduce non-manufacturing timeline work-days	
5	E-commerce	Implement e-commerce for major business segment	$11.04 MM TVM**
6	Purchasing	Improve management***	NQ
6	Accounts payable	Improve management***	$725,000
7	Labor costs	Change plant location	$2 MM
7	Progress payments	Enforce established rules	$2.8 MM
7	Payroll	Improve management***	$60,000
8	Sales financing	Institute program	$1 MM
9	Invoicing	Introduce electronic invoicing	$100,000
10	Collections	Introduce lockboxing	$420,000
10	Collections	Introduce electronic funds transfer	NQ
11	Bank balances	Eliminate tiered concentration	$100,000
11	Bank fees	Reduce pricing and number of banks used	$280,000
	TOTAL		$22.9 MM

NQ = not quantified. MM = millions.

*This benefit comprises cash savings (after-tax interest costs) and non-cash savings (shareholder required returns on common stock).
**Calculated on a ledger basis as $240 million times the final ROS% of 10.5% less the original ROS% of 6.5%, or $9.60 million; and on a TVM basis as $240 million times the ROS% of 9.0% less the original ROS% of 4.4%, or $11.04 million. For ROS %s, see Chapters 4 and 5.
***For specific recommendations, see the appropriate chapter.
^Based on ledger transaction finance benefits.

bidding for purchases, hedging commodities prices, keeping diaries of payables to appropriate payment release dates, implementing a procurement card program, and using direct deposit for payroll.

Other Considerations

Labor expense was examined according to the relative cost of specific plant locations, with specific recommendations regarding high cost facilities. Progress payment costs were reviewed, and mandatory rules were suggested on the basis of the current costs of payment slippage. The advantages of a sales financing program were considered, and the decision was made to outsource to a financial institution. E-commerce invoicing was examined, and a program was initiated for automated data capture and electronic billing through a simplified system. Banking arrangements were reviewed, and various changes were recommended, including lockboxing, the elimination of redundant accounts, and a reduction in bank balances and fees.

Lessons for New Economy Success

Smart's success results from coordinated efforts to improve Gyzmo's performance.

Dismantling Silos

Smart outflanked old silo segments to create a unified, cooperating organization. Each time there was potential resistance to a remedial action, he did three things to assure success:

1. His team developed sufficient facts and analysis to make a clear argument for a course of action.
2. He presented the recommendation to the senior management team, answered their objections, and obtained their agreement.
3. He persuaded the senior managers to sell the action to their organizations and used their positions to create a "change" environment.

Functional assignments will likely be used for the foreseeable future by organizations to manage assets and people. The danger is that those assignments often take on a life of their own, restricting communication and driving analysis of business opportunities for the function's objectives, rather than the goals of the business. One Gyzmo example is the decision to prepare invoices at the convenience of the Information Systems Department rather than on the basis of the company's interests; see Chapter 4.

Performing Comprehensive Financial Reviews

Smart forced Gyzmo to re-examine every aspect of its financial life, including functions normally not subject to such close review. This scrutiny will become a component of business success in the new economy because of the rising cost of capital. We began this book with a discussion of debt and equity financing costs, and their impact on actual results, whether measured as GM, ROS, or ROE. We have seen that financial concerns pervade nearly every part of corporate life and that accurate data on the transaction will drive the future viability of the e-commerce, new economy company.

The transaction finance procedures described in Chapter 4 involve the calculation of the imputed interest cost attributable to the work-days required to complete each manufacturing and marketing activity. Discovering work-day delays allows management to trace the causes, to eliminate inefficiencies, and to improve time value of money returns. This effort requires a thorough investigation of all elements of the cost structure for each business segment, which involves finance in areas previously considered as outside its customary expertise.

Applying Technology

Smart encouraged the selective and thoughtful application of technology to Gyzmo's business needs. Although real-time e-commerce transactions are technically feasible, there is a serious failure risk from uninformed, costly decisions made under time and deal pressures. The situation investigated by Smart and his team showed that the company's capability for managerial and financial analyses and decision-making was significantly less sophisticated than the technology of e-commerce. In the wrong hands, profitability would have been an even greater challenge than in the paper transaction, old economy. Technology can benefit the corporation, but only within a sound business structure.

Finance Transformation in the Real World

Gyzmo is a fictionalized case based on several of our client experiences. There have been only a limited number of actual situations where a company has dismantled silos, conducted comprehensive financial reviews, and successfully applied e-commerce technology.[1] The leading example is General Electric, almost certainly the most successful post–World War II U.S. corporation in terms of improvement in shareholder value.[2]

Management Style

GE has dismantled silos by eliminating layers of managerial bureaucracy, using such venues as employee meetings with CEO Jack Welch and managerial interaction through a variety of discussion groups (e.g., corporate executive councils, work-out meetings, functional councils, and other forums). The form of organization has responded to the needs of each business. For example, GE Capital has decentralized to permit financing and profitability measurement to flow expeditiously to its growth business. Corporate practices have been globalized with acquisitions of sources of supply, penetration into international markets, and the exchange of manager intelligence.

Welch has encouraged business lines to outsource or cooperate in providing non-core activities. This not only produces the function more efficiently than if handled internally (and in some cases creates a new profitable business), it forces different GE managers to

1. In addition to General Electric (GE) discussed in this section, other companies that could be cited include Johnson & Johnson, Dow Chemical, Union Carbide, Ford Motor, Hewlett-Packard, and Citigroup. However, most observers agree that GE is the most successful and most admired company in terms of shareholder value, profitability, globalization, new strategy implementation, and corporate responsibility.
2. Material on GE has been assembled from various sources, including: Tim Smart, "A Day of Reckoning for Bean Counters," *Business Week*, March 14, 1994, pp. 75–76; John Curran, "GE Capital: Jack Welch's Secret Weapon," *Fortune*, November 10, 1997, pp. 116–118; John A. Byrne, "How Jack Welch Runs GE," *Business Week*, June 8, 1998, pp. 90–95; Robert Slater, *Jack Welch and the GE Way: Management Insights and Leadership Secrets of the Legendary CEO*, McGraw-Hill, 1998; Noel Tichy, *Control Your Destiny—Or Someone Else Will*, HarperBusiness, 1999; Thomas A. Stewart, "See Jack. See Jack Run Europe," *Fortune*, September 29, 1999, pp. 124–127; Geoffrey Colvin, "The Ultimate Manager," *Fortune*, November 22, 1999, pp. 185–187; and Srikumar S. Rao, "General Electric, Software Vendor," *Forbes*, January 24, 2000, pp. 144–146.

communicate to develop new approaches. This approach to business is evident in purchasing, customer service, and Internet technology practices at GE. The silos of the pre-Welch years have been replaced with cross-company discussion, idea sharing, and communications.

Finance

The financial system has been completely redesigned to accommodate the inherent strengths of GE's businesses. Each of the various products and services follows its own cycle, allowing diversification and the minimization of enterprise risk. While this concept has precedents as far back as Royal Little's Textron and Harold Geneen's ITT, Welch has leveraged the ability of GE to raise funds at a very low cost of capital with GE Capital's higher-risk commercial finance clients, many of whom would not be particularly appealing to traditional lenders.

Furthermore, manufacturing and non-manufacturing work processes have been analyzed, studied, and re-engineered to develop internal efficiencies. GE has advocated the use of the quality program Six Sigma (see Chapter 7). The result has been the initiation of thousands of projects to cut costs and mistakes, enhance productivity, and eliminate the need for investment in new plants and equipment. Moreover, GE has developed measures to calculate productivity from the intelligent use of existing plants and equipment (as opposed to additional capital expenditures), such as increased inventory cycles and faster integration of acquisitions. GE estimates that it saved some $5 billion through the year 2000.

E-Commerce Technology

Welch has been a strong advocate of e-commerce, and required all major GE businesses to develop and initiate an Internet strategy by the beginning of 2000.[3] Because of an infrastructure that fosters management interaction, teams and ad hoc groups of engineers de-

3. The material in this section is drawn from "Why the Productivity Revolution Will Spread," *Business Week*, February 14, 2000, pp. 112–118, and Douglas Frantz, "To Put G.E. Online Meant Putting a Dozen Industries Online," *New York Times*, March 29, 2000, p. H29.

veloped Internet communications to discuss products under development, while corporate and retail customers access accounts, make purchases, determine the status of their orders, and obtain technical assistance. For example, GE Power Systems uses interactive technology to allow customers and GE engineers to meet on the Web to review plans and designs, make changes, catch errors, and review project costs and timing.

A particularly innovative development has been the creation of a global information-sharing site (WebCity) for GE personnel to exchange ideas and information without on-site visits, travel, and time-zone delays. Purchasing and other more "traditional" Internet functions are also available, and costs of transacting business have been greatly reduced for both GE and for-fee users of the company's Websites. GE estimates that its time to develop products has been reduced by 20% through its e-commerce applications.

Welch also realizes that GE cannot innovate and commercialize all new economy development. Through GE Capital, the company has made significant investments in Internet stocks and other technology-based businesses. According to one analysis, GE has about $4 billion in unrealized gains in publicly traded technology stocks and a position in private investments in the billions of dollars.[4]

Winners and Losers

In either the old or the new economy, the greatest theoretical profit potential will always be in the long-run control of a market, with other sellers unable to compete. However, superoligopolies (cartels) or monopolies have been illegal under the Sherman and Clayton Acts since the end of the nineteenth century. The rigorous prosecution of Microsoft by the U.S. Department of Justice clearly indicates that antitrust will continue to be national policy, and that monopolistic market control will not be allowed to develop.[5] (However, our discussion

4. Andrew Bary, "Juggling Jack," *Barron's*, April 1, 2000, pp. 17–18.
5. See "Conclusions of Law," in *U.S. vs. Microsoft* (2000), Civil Action 98–1232/1233, U.S. District Court for the District of Columbia, summarized in "Company Found to Have Abused Monopoly Power," *New York Times*, April 4, 2000, pp. C14-C15. Judge Thomas Penfield Jackson found that Microsoft monopolized the market for operating systems by mounting ". . . a deliberate assault upon entrepreneurial efforts that . . . could well have enabled the introduction of competition . . ." (at Section

of the impact of e-commerce on industrial concentration, as well as the duration of the Microsoft case, may be prescient regarding future prosecutions by the Justice Department.)

Internet Sites and Search Engines

New economy companies will pursue a strategy, allowable under antitrust law, of broad market penetration and capture by selling at or near cost to secure market share. In the old economy, in contrast, winners generated profits by either achieving limited market penetration at premium prices (e.g., Cadillac) or by attaining broader sales at competitive prices (e.g., Chevrolet).

We commented on oligopoly in Chapter 2, and that structure will continue to dominate industry sectors.

- The control of markets by oligopolies allows strategic positioning for Internet hubs (defined in Chapter 6), as currently seen in steel (through Metalsite), energy (through Altra Energy and HoustonStreet.com), and chemicals (through Chem-Connect and CheMatch).[6]
- Industries in oligopsony, where a few buyers command prices and quantities, will be led by companies such as the large automakers, aerospace companies,[7] and retail chains (e.g., Wal-Mart[8] and Sears[9]).

I.A.III.C., p. C15). Furthermore, the company attempted to collude with Netscape to stop the development of a competitive operating system to Windows; tied its Internet Explorer product to Windows; and engaged in predatory pricing to assure the market dominance of Explorer.

6. FreeMarketsOnline has established a business providing Internet auctions in 40 industries for suppliers of semi-standard manufacturing parts. See the discussion of e-commerce purchasing in William A. Sahlman, "The New Economy Is Stronger Than You Think," *Harvard Business Review*, Vol. 77, November–December 1999, pp. 99–106.
7. See, Keith Bradsher, "Carmakers to Buy Parts on Internet," *New York Times*, February 26, 2000, pp. A1, C14; "Aerospace Companies in Internet Pact," *New York Times*, March 29, 2000, p. C2.
8. Wal-Mart Stores Inc. (WMT), the ultimate retail channel-master, pushes its suppliers to take over costly warehousing and shipping. "The Supply Chain: Leapfrogging a Few Links," *Business Week*, June 28, 1998, pp. 140–142.
9. Sears has announced an Internet exchange in partnership with the French retailer Carrefour. "E-Malls for Business," *Business Week*, March 13, 2000, pp. 32–34.

- Industries of fragmented buyers and sellers, including agriculture, transportation, and construction, will likely default to control by the technology companies.

Similar to the competitive environment in the old economy, a successful hub or exchange will have to offer more than products. Buyers will be looking for advice and direction to product solutions to specific needs or problems, which in turn will require specialized industry knowledge.

The standard prototype for new economy strategy is Amazon.com, which has seriously eroded the competitive position of the traditional retail bookseller. However, Amazon has not generated any earnings as of 2001, and there is no assurance that it can capitalize on its position as a bookseller and extend its reach to sell other products successfully. There is certainly no indication that this strategy will be generally applicable to e-commerce markets. Even if it is, it will most likely be accomplished by partnering, strategic alliances, and "co-opetition,"since it is unlikely that any one participant can economically or legally control an entire market.

The stock market may not come to recognize this situation for several years, allowing the prices of new economy stocks, including Internet companies, to rise on the basis of expectations for future market capture, rather than real earnings. As one example, Digital Lightwave, a company that produces Internet fiber-optic cable, had a market value of $1.8 billion (in early 2000) on sales of $50 million and sold at about 150 times earnings![10] In this environment, quarterly profit reports are not very meaningful, as we have seen with the recent valuations of technology stocks that have nominal or no earnings.

New Economy Profits

The real impact of the new economy—ignored by most observers—will be to make old profitability metrics obsolete. Inefficiencies previously hidden by averaging profitable and unprofitable customers, products, and transactions will overwhelm old economy companies. In this environment it will be difficult to manage against return-on-

10. Cited in "How High Is Too High for Stocks That Lead a Business Revolution?" *The Wall Street Journal*, January 10, 2000, pp. A1, A14.

equity targets, and there will be significant shortfalls in earnings and stock market performance. The change will affect old and new economy companies, those in the Fortune 500 and those hoping for $50 million in annual sales, those in the U.S. and those in other regions of the world, those in industries that provide essential products and those that hope to find a market.

Looking at the Gyzmo situation, we find that the benefits it can gain in the new economy derive from various sources. It is difficult to separate the benefits of e-commerce from other factors because of the close interrelationship between electronic and business initiatives.[11] If we assign the share of benefits derived to each general type of recommendation, we get the following:

Transaction finance	42%
Timeline efficiencies	33%
Capital structure	25%

In other words, more than two-fifths of all of the benefits developed for Gyzmo were derived from transaction finance. Assuming that Gyzmo—a composite drawn from our experiences with real companies—is representative of industry in general, we have to pay very close attention to work-day delays and to the inefficiencies that result from them.

New Economy Pitfalls

Beyond these financial considerations, we also have to consider the unique demands of the new economy.

• *Our counterparties may be strangers.* We may not know who our vendors or customers are in an e-commerce world. Bids will be offered or sought by electronic messages from global sources and users. Credit-worthiness reviews and enforceable guarantees will be required to assure counterparties' performance.

• *We may agree to transactions that cannot be completed.* The e-commerce requirement for rapid response will inevitably cause poor

11. The need to integrate e-commerce and business strategy is noted with reference to five companies in Marcia Stepanek, "How to Jump-Start Your E-Strategy," *Business Week*, June 5, 2000, pp. EB 95–100.

decision-making, low profits or losses, and the failure to deliver product on time and to the expected standard of quality.

• *We may increase our exposure to legal action.* Old economy etiquette between friendly buyers and sellers will diminish, and a failure to deliver on agreed terms will lead to threats, severe penalties, and lawsuits.

Who Will Be the Big Winners?

The big winners—old or new economy—are companies that adjust their accounting and financial calculations to the requirements of a real-time environment. As we determined in the Gyzmo case, they will increase their profits by perhaps one-third to one-half through such actions, depending on their current degree of efficiency. Such companies will secure a market position that their competitors will be unable to challenge without heroic efforts.

These winners will come from the old and from the new economies, involving the sale of various products and services, manufactured and outsourced, to customers in traditional distribution channels and through e-commerce, in the U.S. and in global markets. These companies will be able to examine the impact of each variable in a business opportunity and decide whether to proceed, amend the terms, or pass.

They will understand where there are potential "slippages" that can cause expected returns to vanish. They will respond quickly to delays, work group problems, raw material delivery or price changes, mediocre manufacturing quality, and any other environmental change. Take another look at Exhibit 3-1. While new economy companies will clearly be successful (as will their stockholders), the biggest *percentage* winners will be those old economy companies that can adjust. *Business Week* formulated a list of six industries that will have big e-commerce successes; see Exhibit 12-2.

Who Will Be the Other Winners?

The moderate winners will be the Internet sites, search engines, and computer hardware and software providers that offer the facilities for this business activity. Fifteen such companies are listed in the appendix. Information intermediaries with broad access to sources of supply and customers have a significant potential for long-term

Exhibit 12-2. Industry winners from total Internet activity (business and consumer).

Industry	1999 Revenue	2003 Revenue	Projected Annual Revenue Growth
Computing and electronics	$53B	$410B	66.8%
Energy	$11B	$170B	98.3%
Financial services	$14B	$80B	54.6%
Retailing	$18B	$108B	56.5%
Telecommunications	$2B	$15B	65.5%
Travel	$13B	$67B	50.7%

B = billions.
Source: Reprinted from "The Internet Age" (special issue), *Business Week,* October 4, 1999, pp. 84–98, by special permission, copyright © 1999 by The McGraw-Hill Companies, Inc.

success. Assuming that compensation arrangements involving such companies will most likely be based on flat fees, the potential revenue stream for all participants could eventually be in the hundreds of millions of dollars.[12]

However, their successes will be moderate, not "home runs." Companies with a major Internet image will retain that presence, with a few new participants attaining significant market share. The "B2B" stock market valuations of the second half of 1999 and early 2000 were never sustainable, and the subsequent collapse in Nasdaq technology sectors could have been predicted. And even when B2B really gets going, not only will revenues to Internet providers be limited by transaction revenues based on competitive fees, there will also be a significant volume of direct selling-business-to-buying-

12. Writing in the *New York Times*, Richard A. Oppel, Jr., takes a contrary view. He believes that cashflow will be calculated as a percentage of the total e-commerce revenue stream, with the potential calculated in the billions of dollars. "The Higher Stakes of Business-to-Business Trade," March 5, 2000, Business Section, p. 3. However, the general consensus appears to support our proposition that the revenues will be based on competitive flat fees; see, for example, Daniel Lyons, "B2B Bluster," *Forbes*, May 1, 2000, pp. 122–126.

business activity. For example, if General Motors chooses to deal directly with its suppliers, intermediaries will see zero revenue.

Who Will Be the Losers?

The losers will be those companies that do not develop an adequate system of financial metrics to provide the necessary insights, that continue to operate their businesses as "silos" with an "us against them" mentality, and that adapt technology mindlessly without consideration for the viability of the organizational structure in which it will be housed. There are numerous examples of such companies scattered through such old economy industries as insurance, packaging, steel, textiles and apparel, and healthcare delivery. Obviously, the losers will also be those companies that choose not to participate in e-commerce.

A Final Warning

Although real-time e-commerce transactions are technologically feasible, there is a serious risk from uninformed, costly decisions made under time and deal pressures. The discoveries of science often precede the acquisition of the human knowledge necessary to intelligently manage those innovations. Certainly, managerial and financial analyses and decision-making capability are significantly less sophisticated than the technology of e-commerce in the new economy, making the achievement of profitability an even greater challenge in the new economy than in the paper transaction, old economy.

Paraphrasing Einstein's words (quoted at the start of this chapter), the new economy has the potential to be a serious menace. To take advantage of e-commerce, we have to learn to bring order to financial management.

Chapter 12 Appendix

ERP AND XML

We reviewed various supply chain/manufacturing concepts in Chapter 7. These developments do not discourage the separation of business functions into "silos," resulting in barriers to integrated planning and profitability information. Utilizing enterprise resource planning (ERP) and extensive markup language (XML) can move a company in the direction of integration of company functions.

ERP

ERP links company information in a computerized system through thousands of data tables. Each table uses a series of decision toggles that direct the software to specific decision paths. The goal is to construct a file structure with sufficient flexibility to enable linkage with or detachment from other company data elements as requirements change.

Many companies have separate computer applications that cannot readily interact. By using a single package, ERP automates the various tasks required to complete essential business processes. For example, it allows the necessary data to reside on the system to complete a customer's order, arrange for credit, determine inventory levels (or the status of work-in-process), and schedule delivery. The leading ERP vendors include SAP, Baan, PeopleSoft, Oracle, and J. D. Edwards. The modules typically offered include financial accounting, treasury and investment management, enterprise planning, order processing, production planning, materials purchasing, human resources, and sales.

There are various difficulties in achieving a satisfactory ERP system.

- Certain resources of an enterprise are often not included in ERP, such as intellectual capital (see Chapter 2), activity-based costing (see Chapter 3), and customer/sales management.
- There may be redundant data tables to meet the requirements of different ERP components, such as organization charts in the human resources module and for customer service inquires in the marketing module.
- Although the anticipation of Y2K resulted in the abandonment or rewriting of legacy systems, there are often remnants of such software throughout many companies. ERP does not conveniently accommodate legacy systems, resulting in extensive re-programming efforts.
- The peculiarities of different companies and industries have impeded successful implementation, as standard business processes are relied on to conform to ERP protocols. The need to change company operations, acquire systems and expertise, and abandon existing procedures can escalate ERP costs into the millions of dollars.

As the result of these problems, some companies have been forced to abandon ERP projects, radically change their business processes, or customize the software (which may result in programming bugs, susceptibility to viruses, and difficulty in future upgrading).

The role of ERP in the new economy remains to be determined. While the potential value of e-commerce is obvious, it is indisputable that a significant limitation is the lack of a standard protocol for communications among customers, vendors, and other market participants. Electronic data interchange (EDI) has been only partially successful as a business communications technique, largely because of the investment required for technology and expertise, with in-place networks limited to 250,000 companies.[13]

XML

In the near future, e-commerce will utilize "extensible markup language" (XML), the replacement communications format for EDI, to

13. EDI was defined in Chapter 2, p. 40.

allow proprietary applications to be interrogated both intra- and intercompany. As an example, an e-commerce system will produce a purchase order in XML and transmit the file electronically to a business partner, whose system will read the purchase order and use the data to enter a new sales order to its order-entry module. The manual entry of the sales-order will be eliminated, and the required time for the transaction will be reduced. In the next decade, XML will be used to access Internet information and business workflow data, such as to obtain customer credit data (e.g, through credit reporting agencies) and to manage customer shipments (e.g., courier tracking data). Company actions and external interfaces, such as credit approval or denial or responses to customer inquiries, will be expedited.[14]

XML is an improvement on the current Website language in general use, HTML, as it provides the opportunity to provide information, through tags embedded in the language, on the meaning of the data displayed. Furthermore, XML is flexible, because programmers are not constrained by a defined language and can define tags as documents are being written. This flexibility is encouraging vendors of application software to develop standard XML configurations for business documents. Counterparties will be able to conduct e-commerce transactions through an XML parser, as long as each understands the meaning of the tags used.

Transaction finance will be facilitated by the use of XML to assist in developing financial records. E-commerce will develop rules (remember the discussion in Chapter 1) to search for meaningful data on elements in the various cycles discussed in Part II, and these data will be accessible in consolidated reports. While delays in manufacturing and non-manufacturing portions of the timeline will inevitably continue to occur, management will be informed promptly of such episodes, and will be able to begin remedial actions promptly.

14. See Stewart McKie, ''Crossing the Chasm,'' *Business Finance*, January 2000, pp. 67–72.

SELECTED MODERATE WINNERS— E-COMMERCE FACILITATORS

Company/symbol/ '99 results	Products	Major competitors/ ROE
Advanced Micro Devices (AMD) Sales = $2,858MM Profits = ($89MM)	Microprocessors (ranks second after Intel); embedded chips; non-volatile memories.	Intel Motorola National Semiconductor ROE = NM
Cisco (CSCO) Sale = $12,154MM Profits = $2,096MM	Internet products that link and power networks, including routers and switches; dial-up access servers; network management software; telecommunications networking. Has established alliances with leading technology companies.	3Com Lucent Nortel Networks ROE = 18%
Compaq (CPQ) Sales = $38,525MM Profits = $569MM	Personal computer manufacturer (ranks no. 1) and computer seller (ranks no. 3 behind IBM and HWP); other products include handheld portable systems, corporate servers, and technology services.	Dell Hewlett-Packard IBM ROE = 4%
Dell (DELL) Sales = $25,265MM Profits = $1,666MM	PC makers and direct-sale computers (ranks no. 1), including hardware and the marketing of third-party software and peripherals, including notebooks, PCs, and network servers; markets a variety of peripherals and software for other manufacturers.	Compaq Gateway IBM ROE = 31%
Hewlett-Packard (HWP) Sales = $48,253MM Profits = $3,491MM	Computers, imaging and printing peripherals, software, and related services (ranks no. 2 behind IBM); becoming an Internet specialist providing Web hardware, software, and support to corporate customers.	Compaq IBM Xerox ROE = 19%

Company	Description	Competitors
IBM (IBM) Sales = $87,548MM Profits = $7,712MM	Computers, including PCs, notebooks, mainframes, and network servers (ranks no. 1); software (ranks no. 2 behind Microsoft); and peripherals; owns software pioneer Lotus Development (Lotus Notes messaging); refocusing on Internet business.	Compaq Hewlett-Packard Microsoft ROE = 38%
Intel (INTC) Sales = $29,389MM Profits = $7,314MM	Semiconductors (ranks no. 1), controlling about 80% of the microprocessor market; makes the powerful Pentium chip and the low-end Celeron chip for IBM-compatible PCs; Intel chips are also used in products for communications, industrial equipment, and the military; pushing into networking services and communications products.	Advanded Micro Devices IBM Motorola ROE = 22%
Intuit (INTU) Sales = $847.6MM Profits = $376.5MM	Financial software, including Quicken personal finance software, QuickBooks small-business tax software, and tax filing application TurboTax; will offer users financial services over the Internet, including payroll, insurance, mortgage processing, and tax and investment information.	ADP H&R Block Microsoft ROE = 19
Microsoft (MSFT) Sales = $19,747MM Profits = $7,785MM	Software (ranked no. 1) although currently in antitrust litigation with the Justice Department; products include the Windows operating systems, MS Office business productivity suite (Excel, Word, PowerPoint), reference works, a Web browser, online services, and an e-commerce portal, MSN (Microsoft Network).	America Online Oracle Sun Microsystems ROE = 27%

Company	Description	Competitors / ROE
Oracle (ORCL) Sales = $9,680MM Profits = $1,910MM	Database management systems software, permitting multiple users and applications to access the same data simultaneously (ranked no. 1); database software supports computers that access programs from the Web; software development tools; resource management applications; consulting, technical support; other services.	IBM Microsoft SAP ROE = 35%
Peoplesoft (PSFT) Sales = $1,429MM Profits = ($178MM)	Designer of business applications across computer networks (ranked no. 2 after SAP); ERP software addresses accounting, manufacturing, supply chain management, inventory, and distribution; industry-specific software for the insurance and utility markets; consulting, training, and support services.	Baan Oracle SAP ROE = NM
Quest (QSFT) Sales = $70.9MM Profits = $3.4MM	Software for corporate computer network and Internet information management, including database diagnostics, network monitoring, capacity planning, application problem detection and resolution, change management, and data replication in the event of system failures.	Actuate Mobius Management Systems Veritas Software ROE = 10%

Company	Description	Competitors
SAP AG (SAP) Sales = $5,240MM Profits = $550MM	Ranked no. 1 in the development of integrated business application software to provide cost-effective comprehensive solutions for businesses; through mySAP.com, provides these products through the Internet.	Peoplesoft Oracle Baan ROE = 23%
Silicon Graphics (SGI) Sales = $2,749MM Profits = $54MM	Manufactures high-end servers; the advanced graphics computers used to create special effects for movies; modeling and animation software and microprocessors.	Hewlett-Packard IBM Sun Microsystems ROE = 4%
Sun Microsystems Sales = $11,726MM Profits = $1,031MM	Produces UNIX-based, workstation computers, storage devices, and servers for corporate computer networks and Web sites; the largest computer manufacturer to use its own chips (SPARC) and operating systems (Solaris); created Java, a programming language intended to create software that can run unchanged on any computer (similar to XML).	Compaq IBM Microsoft ROE = 21%

MM = millions
NM = not meaningful

Sources: For company descriptions, Hoover's (www.hoovers.com); for 1999 financials, Hoover's and the *Fortune Magazine* Fortune 500 issue, April 17, 2000. Information supplemented by company Websites. A comprehensive listing of e-commerce companies may be found in the "Information Technology Annual Report," *Business Week,* June 19, 2000, pp. 73–160.

Bibliography of E-Commerce and New Economy Books

The New Economy

Boulton, Richard E. S., Barry D. Libert, and Steve M. Samek. *Cracking the Value Code*. New York: HarperBusiness, 2000.

Brown, John Seely, and Paul Duguid. *The Social Life of Information*. Boston: Harvard Business School Press, 2000.

Coyle, Diane. *The Weightless World*. Cambridge, Mass.: MIT Press, 1998.

Davis, Stanley M., and Christopher Meyer. *Future Wealth*. Boston: Harvard Business School Press, 2000.

Evans, Philip, and Thomas S. Wurster. *Blown to Bits*. Boston: Harvard Business School Press, 1999.

Herzenberg, Stephen A., John A. Alic, and Howard Wial. *New Rules for a New Economy*. Ithaca, N.Y.: Cornell University Press, 1998.

Kelly, Kevin. *New Rules for the New Economy*. New York: Viking, 1998.

E-Commerce Strategy

Aldrich, Douglas F. *Mastering the Digital Marketplace*. New York: John Wiley & Sons, 1999.

Aron, Daniel. *The E-Business (R)evolution*. Palo Alto, Calif.: Hewlett-Packard Professional Books, 2000.

Camp, L. Jean. *Trust and Risk in Internet Commerce*. Cambridge, Mass.: MIT Press, 1999.

Chase, Larry. *Essential Business Tactics for the Net*. New York: John Wiley & Sons, 1998.

Fellenstein, Craig, and Ron Wood. *Exploring E-Commerce*. Englewood Cliffs, N.J.: Prentice-Hall, 1999.

Gutterman, Alan S., et al. *The Professional's Guide to Doing Business on the Internet, 2000*. New York: Harcourt Brace, 1999.

Korper, Steffano, et al. *The E-Commerce Book: Building the E-Empire*. San Diego: Academic Press, 1999.

Leebaert, Derek (ed.). *The Future of the Electronic Marketplace*. Cambridge, Mass.: MIT Press, 1999.

May, Paul. *The Business of E-Commerce*. Cambridge, Mass.: Cambridge University Press, 2000.

Price Waterhouse Coopers et al. *Executive's Guide to E-Commerce*. New York: John Wiley & Sons, 1999.

Rosen, Anita. *The E-Commerce Question and Answer Book: A Survival Guide for Business Managers*. New York: AMACOM, 1999.

Rosenoer, Jonathan, et al. *The Clickable Corporation: Successful Strategies for Capturing the Internet Advantage*. New York: Free Press, 1999.

Schwartz, Evan I. *Digital Darwinism: 7 Breakthrough Business Strategies for Surviving in the Cutthroat Web Economy*. New York: Broadway Books, 1999.

Siebel, Thomas M., et al. *Cyber Rules: Strategies for Excelling at E-Business*. New York: Doubleday, 1999.

Siegel, David. *Futurize Your Enterprise: Business Strategy in the Age of the E-Customer*. New York: John Wiley & Sons, 1999.

Tapscott, Don (ed.). *Creating Value in the Network Economy*. Boston: Harvard Business School Press, 1999.

Tapscott, Don, et al. (eds.). *Blueprint to the Digital Economy: Wealth Creation in the Era of E-Business*. New York: McGraw-Hill, 1998.

Westland, J. Christopher, and Theodore H. K. Clark. *Global Electronic Commerce: Theory and Cases*. Cambridge, Mass.: MIT Press, 1999.

Windham, Laurie, et al. *Dead Ahead: The Web Dilemma and the New Rules of Business*. New York: Allworth, 1999.

Law and Regulation

Hance, Olivier, et al. *Business & Law on the Internet*. New York: McGraw-Hill, 1997.

Johnston, David, et al. *Cyberlaw: What You Need to Know About Doing Business Online*. Toronto: Stoddart, 1997.

Business Planning

Ezor, Jonathan I. *Clicking Through: A Survival Guide for Bringing Your Company Online*. Princeton, N.J.: Bloomberg Press, 1999.

Kalakota, Ravi, et al. *E-Business: Roadmap for Success*. Reading, Mass.: Addison-Wesley, 1999.

Maddox, Kate, and Dana Blankenhorn. *Web Commerce: Building a Digital Business*. New York: John Wiley & Sons, 1998.

Rich, Jason R. *The Unofficial Guide to Starting a Business Online*. New York: IDG Books Worldwide, 1999.

Romm, Celia T., and Fay Sudweeks (eds.). *Doing Business Electronically: A Global Perspective of Electronic Commerce*. New York: Springer-Verlag, 1998.

Ross, L. Manning. *businessplan.com: how to write a web-woven strategic business plan*. Grants Pass, Oreg.: PSI Research, 1998.

Schwartz, Evan I. *Webonomics: Nine Essential Principles for Growing Your Business on the World Wide Web*. New York: Bantam-Double-day-Dell, 1998.

Seybold, Patricia B., et al. *Customers.Com: How to Create a Profitable Business Strategy for the Internet and Beyond*. New York: Times Books, 1998.

Timmers, Paul. *Electronic Commerce: Strategies and Models for Business-to-Business Trading*. New York: John Wiley & Sons, 1999.

Payment Risk and Economic Analysis

Whinston, Andrew B., et al. *The Economics of Electronic Commerce*. New York: Macmillan, 1997.

INDEX